Focused, Fit, and Fulfilled After 50!

Michelle Baker

For my pack.

You know who you are.

Much love.

ACKNOWLEDGMENTS

Writing my first book was a wonderful adventure, and I have so many individuals to thank for encouraging me along the way. To my son Andrew, who patiently listened every time I had a fresh idea and who helped me test drive many of the health and fitness concepts listed in this book. I love you! To my dear friend Andrea, who was always there to hear about my big dreams, providing inspiration when I felt I was losing steam. Her support and faith kept me going throughout the process. To my *vecina* Jennifer and her daughters Brittny, Jodi, and Ariana, who care for my family unconditionally and always laugh at my jokes. To my incredible Aunt Sue, whose genuine interest in what is going on in my life is always so appreciated.

To the many life and fitness coaches that have crossed my path over the years, including Raffaella and Marie, who I met at sea and who each made a lasting impact on my approach to mindfulness. And to the business mentors too numerous to list who have impacted my life and ability to lead.

To my talented editors Rebecca and Linda of Cup and Quill Services for Writers. I felt supported and uplifted from our very first phone call and feel incredibly grateful for your heartfelt connection and feedback.

To Nova, who is always by my side, and to the Ravens, who remind me to look up.

Finally, to my wonderful parents Albert and Patricia, who made me the dreamer that I am today. Your love, guidance, and faith in my ability made this all possible.

Much love.

Michelle

TABLE OF CONTENTS

Introduction

Plateaus suck.

I have no idea how I made such good friends with my plateau, much less how this sneaky bastard pulled me into its vortex of emptiness. But I was there: fifty-four years old, losing steam, listening to the alluring siren calls of comfort and control. Comfort, as in, "I just want a little break, some time to rest and regroup." Control, as if "getting organized and checking off my all-important to-do list" would unlock some magical door to inner peace. Because truth be told, that's what I wanted. A little peace. Peace of mind, peace of soul, or maybe just some peace and quiet. This malfunctioning mindset led me to the dreary, monotonous ledge I was sitting on, waiting for amazing things to happen *to* me. Have you ever been there? Not exactly the birthplace of inspiration.

I was right smack-dab in the middle of my own personal plateau, and that awful feeling of being "stuck" permeated every aspect of my life. I was tediously treading water from a weight perspective, hovering between "kind of in shape, kind of not," despite a wide variety of new routines designed to take me to the next level. The same went for my ability to focus on the nearly uninterrupted flow of new goals, fresh ideas, and big dreams that streamed into my consciousness. I would grab onto each one and feel the beauty of the notion, seeing with clarity a vision of a new and inspiring future, a new and exciting version of me. Gravity always beckoned, however, and once again, I found myself passively watching my "other commitments" (aka my routine) draw me back into the present reality. My level of happiness mirrored all the above. I was content, sure, and had moments of exhilaration following an event or cool moment, but it never lasted, and soon enough, I would resume my habitation on the comfortable ledge that existed between the past and anything exciting or new.

That was my reality for a while, stuck in neutral, spinning my wheels. My plateau, also known as a "state of little or no change," was not, by nature, evil or even wrong, and it wasn't out to get me. On the contrary, I believe it was trying to protect me from the seemingly malevolent vibrations of disappointment, failure, and fatigue. My present was a safe, known entity, a slow, predictable series of days filled with minor deviations and controllable variances that sometimes added a little flavor to my life experience. Plateaus are like that comfortable, inviting bench you find after a long walk, a place to sit for a spell and rest your tired feet and restive soul. After all, you've been pushing hard for a while now and deserve a break, don't you?

Unfortunately, those innocent respites often lulled me into a trance, and I began to believe words like "comfort" and "routine" belonged on the road to happiness. That a quiet night or two was just what the doctor ordered. *"A few nights off from time to time is refreshing,"* the plateau encouraged, *"and now is a great time to watch Madam Secretary again. You can get back on track tomorrow!"*

A few quiet nights turned into years of sub-par, routine, and simply adequate days. My once steady fitness lifestyle diminished into occasional bursts of energy, usually centered around a new exercise routine, an innovative gym, or the latest "guaranteed to work" diet. My focus was all over the place, jumping into every shiny penny concept that promised "real results." The magic bullet never materialized, and after a while, I was tired, soft, and directionless. While my full-time corporate job felt like an area of solid contribution, even there I felt I could do more. I was over fifty, losing focus, unfit, and desperately seeking some form of real fulfillment.

I thought I was doing all the right things to employ authentic change. I read the right material and feverishly studied all the best mindset and fitness scholars looking for the answer. And I did find solutions, repeatedly! Most of today's premiere thinkers are brilliant! Knowing *what* to do was never the problem, and motivation wasn't an issue either. I have a strong work ethic, a drive to succeed and contribute, and I don't think anyone would ever describe me as a slacker. It's not that I was sitting around eating proverbial bonbons. I was just ***stuck***. I had the career, the family, the shiny new car, and some "ride or die" friends; however, I was plagued with a constant sensation of "searching" that bordered on desperation. What was missing in my life? Why was I not more grateful for what I already had and the opportunities that were presented to me? What was absent? I had no clue.

Until one day I did. Have you ever experienced an "epiphany?" A feeling of such profound clarity that you felt like your thoughts were coming from somewhere else, a source beyond rational consciousness? I have, and the epiphany that helped me make this dramatic shift started on a 3-hour flight to Houston in February of 2019. Traveling for work, I sat there in row twenty-one, internally debating about whether I should spend the time dutifully answering emails, reading the book I had brought onboard, or watching a movie on the nine-inch screen in front of me. Instead, I found myself drinking a cup of hot coffee with two dairy-free creamers, blissfully staring into magnificent white clouds through my over-wing window seat. Whether it was the coffee, the serenity of flight, or a combination of the two, ideas of stunning clarity started pouring through me. One exhilarating thought led to another. These led to the next concept about change, accountability, goals I could achieve, and massive shifts that would come into my life. The inspired thoughts seemed to be flooding, uninhibited, directly from my subconscious into my fully "woke" conscious self. It felt amazing!

Not having a pen or paper available, I typed into the notes section of my phone, two thumbs flying across the screen nearly as fast as the stream of thoughts were generating. It was a pure, uninterrupted flow of ideas that I didn't dare stop, terrified I would lose the thread and miss out on something important. Occasionally, I put the phone down, rested my thumbs, and stared into the clouds again. Each time I did, a new hypothesis, or a fresh iteration of the original idea, glided into my consciousness and demanded to be recognized and recorded. I wrote during the entire flight, other than the few moments where I paused to breathe in and recognize the magic of the moment. I felt the vibration of the epiphany in my body and knew that it WAS an epiphany. I also understood, with all that I am, that this stream of consciousness would change my life.

What was this earth-shaking, magical torrent of awareness? It was the visualization of the concept introduced and extrapolated throughout the chapters of this book. I saw, felt, and embodied the interrelated harmony of **Focus**, **Fitness,** and **Fulfillment**. I saw myself energized, in peak shape, and focused on new goals that made life enticing and rewarding. A level of joy and satisfaction that I had never experienced before accompanied this vision, and it was all right there amongst the tiny misspelled words on my iPhone.

I envisioned this book helping others find clarity, health, and fulfillment, breaking through old habits and beliefs that just didn't serve them anymore. I also saw working personally with individuals who needed an advocate to stand by them as they navigated through the process. Together we would create a ripple effect of massive change! I knew I had to get these words on paper, and I appreciated the pure current in which they arrived. Those moments of clarity and flow can be encouraged, but they can't be forced or coerced. When they come, you must place them in fertile soil quickly and dedicate time to watch them expand and grow. That's exactly what I did.

The Premise

The principle that struck me like lightning, (figuratively, of course, since we were cruising at 35,000 feet), was that to achieve *any* goal I needed to find an abundant reservoir of two critical resources: **Time** and **Energy**. During the time when I received the idea for this book I was already, ostensibly, at capacity on both. (It turns out that was NOT true! But we'll get to that later.) I worked full-time as a leader in a Fortune 100 company, frequently traveled for business, and took care of most of the tasks of family life. I was also in the middle of a demanding MBA with just over a year of studies left. How in the world would I carve out time to pursue a distinctively different path? I barely had enough time and energy to navigate the water I was in! The key was an essential shift in my beliefs and behaviors, and it started with this concept: if I radically improved my level of health and *Fitness*, I would improve my ability to *Focus*, better directing my energy, thoughts, and attention, which should, in theory, profoundly enhance and sustain my level of *Fulfillment* and joy!

It was simple, clear, and incredibly captivating. *"That's it!"* my inner being kept screaming, *"That's the real deal!"* I was climbing up a new mountain, fueled by enthusiasm for a concept I felt was a winner. What I didn't know was that one critical component was still missing, and without it that damn plateau would keep a bungee cord wrapped securely around my waist, ready to snap me back. *"Venture out and play with your new idea,"* the ledge encouraged, *"I'll be right here waiting when the notion burns itself out."* Damn. Was I destined to be anchored forever to my present reality? Was a new beginning, at my age, an unrealistic adventure, cherished by many, reserved for the few? Have you ever felt that sense of doubt and disappointment?

The Catalyst for ALL Change

Once I realized that something was truly missing from my epiphany-fueled plans I immediately sought resolution. However, it was not as simple as running down to Whole Foods and purchasing the ambiguous ingredient, googling for answers on the Web, or looking for the highest-rated "fix" on Amazon. This deficit was deeply personal, and no other soul on earth could help me. What was this elusive, self-centered puzzle piece?

A goal. Not just "a goal," but THE goal. The *"why"* behind how this time I HAD to change, no excuses would be allowed.

Something that would get me off the ledge of comfort and up the mountain in earnest, cutting off all paths except the one that led straight up. The realization hit the center of my being in such a profound way that I immediately understood that I had found the solution, the truth, the key. *I had to determine my empowering "why" to create massive, sustainable change.*

I already had a considerable goal in mind, but I needed to peel back the onion a few layers to discover what it really meant. Originally, I thought the objective was a physical thing, something tangible and solid. In my case, that *thing* is a beautiful horse farm, with lots of land, a quiet home, and a barn that is as functional as it is picturesque. My happiest memories of childhood are attached to our days living in the country, and I have long held the belief that someday I would own a farm of my own. I had this dream for quite a while, though, so initially, I was curious why it had not previously incited me to new heights and shifted my less than ideal paradigms (belief systems). Why not, and why now? Because the physical manifestation of the farm was not my true goal or my deep-seated, soul-enticing reason for change. What I desired was a feeling: *the sensation of being home.*

I have been a nomad for a long time, moving from state to state, surrounding myself with busy-ness, and trying to fill the unidentified gap in my being. The gap was the feeling of belonging, a place to dig deep roots, a foundation for the next "*I'm fifty, but far from done*" chapters. Once I grasped this concept, I had no doubt that the realization of my dream was worth changing *everything*. I finally had my big dream to pursue AND the compelling reason behind it!

> *"Finally think I found what I'm chasing after."*
>
> – "Alive" by Krewella

Always A Nomad, Never the Mayor

For those of you who are wondering why the feeling of home is so elusive to me, I would love to explain the thought a bit more before moving on. You may even be thinking, "Then buy a house already. Don't you have a good job?" I do, but that's not the point or the feeling that's missing.

I grew up in a loving, "normal," middle-class family. My brothers and I were close, and I was fortunate to always be surrounded by animals and sports, two things I will always cherish. There was one aspect of my life, however, that was anything but "normal." We moved almost every year! Ping-ponging between the comfort of the suburbs, and the peace and tranquility of a place in the country, it felt like we were always packing boxes and looking forward to what was next. My dad had a great job with Kodak, back when Kodak was one of the most recognized and reliable brands in the country, and my mom was a well-respected nurse in Rochester, New York. It wasn't their careers that caused these moves. It was the same restless spirit that I feel today, and certainly felt in the years leading up to this book. *"This next place will be better, and you kids are going to love it,"* my dad would promise. *"This time we are going to make it our own, grow some roots, and stay for a while."* Some call this "destination addiction," the idea that the next place, job, or home will make everything right. My entire family experienced that one in spades!

Unfortunately, the roots never materialized, and we continued the quest for a real "home" until I was sixteen and left the house. All in all I attended twelve different schools between kindergarten and high school graduation, and that prevalence of sustained upheaval has played in my longing for personal roots. No regrets, though. I have a wonderful family whom I love, and we are all close because of this shared history. My brothers are dear friends, I have wonderful memories of my grandparents, and my mom and dad are still a part of my core and who I turned out to be. I was simply unable to achieve that deep-seated sensation of being home.

To clarify, I have lived in "houses" for most of my adult life, initially with amazing friends, and eventually in places I owned. I raised my son Andrew in Central Florida and had three different domiciles during that period. Yet even with a great cement block house in a cool neighborhood I couldn't fight the restlessness inside. They were all lovely houses and served their purpose, but nothing really screamed "the roots of forever." Not one of them gave me the peace of knowing "This is mine. This is *me!*" I know today that the reason for this was that my soul was searching, still, for a place to call home.

A Glimpse in Tennessee and New York

I experienced a fleeting sensation of "home" when I had the privilege of moving to a beautiful horse farm in Tennessee in 2011. The serenity, open spaces, and hard work that is congruent with living on a working ranch gave me ephemeral moments of fulfillment and joy. Unfortunately, work and financial stressors dominated that period, so it was nearly impossible to immerse myself in the practice of being present and appreciative. The roots never took, and two years later, I was a nomad once again.

I also had moments of centered belonging in 2017, when on a scattered whim I bought a small, cute as can be, two-bedroom Cape Cod-style house in Rochester near my mom. I loved that little gem and immediately furnished the place and set it up for future use. I couldn't stop smiling! I never had the chance to live there full-time, however, as I worked in California and could only fly back and forth on occasion. It did provide a temporary landing spot for my pack (Andrew and Nova, our rescue dog) while I traveled the country, and for that I am eternally grateful. I sold the house at the peak of the seller's market in 2018 and at least made my money back.

In hindsight, and what I believe is the silver lining in all of this, is that the feeling of the ranch in Tennessee, and the house in Rochester, combined to cement the physical representation of what I was looking for. Maybe my "home" would be a horse farm, near my family, in Upstate New York. Maybe it was a return to Florida where my dad and brothers still live. Either way, perhaps it was time to go home after all. At the very least I was thrilled with the feelings the clarified intentions were producing.

"I spent twenty years trying to get out of this place.
I was looking for something I couldn't replace."
   – "Who Says You Can't Go Home?" Bon Jovi

The Triad Concept

As I let this new realization permeate my being, it was time to test the premise of my epiphany and define it for future use. Ultimately, I sought to prove that through this proposition I had:

1. The ability to clear away the mental clutter and pervasive noise and **Focus** on what was important.

2. A desire to honor the body by significantly reducing unhealthy foods, toxins, beliefs, and habits that did not serve it. In addition, it provided a way to break through workout "ruts" and create a lifestyle that would lead to peak levels of **Fitness**.

3. A method to reduce the negative influence of the past while achieving joy and **Fulfillment** in the here and now. Reliving previous events, feeling regret for unsuccessful fitness attempts, failed relationships, or missed goals would not move anyone into a compelling future. That's how people get "stuck"! By significantly reducing the amount of time spent reliving old memories we can plant one foot firmly in the

miraculous present, while sliding a few toes into a compelling future!

As I write these words, I am fifty-four years young and, through the concepts introduced in this book, have achieved higher levels of focus and fitness than I have seen in decades. I completely transformed my approach to exercise and eating and have enough mental energy to still hold the full-time leadership role, study for that MBA, and write this book. Peak energy certainly has its perks! I also feel more consistently centered and fulfilled than at any other period in my five-decade journey on this earth so far! I feel like I am traveling the early miles of an exciting road trip, car packed and ready to go, a new playlist (created just for the trip!) jamming in the background. I have one of the most soul-captivating goals I have ever had pulling me forward and fueling the journey. My goal has seeped into my being, lighting the darkest of my doubts and reinvigorating a passion for life that is simply intoxicating.

This book is layered with deeply personal stories, as that is the only way I can think to share how it happened for me. My hope is that you can take some nugget of truth from these writings, picking out something that resonates with you, some connection we may have that helps you break through any self-imposed ceiling on your hopes and dreams.

When you can feel in your soul that there is so much more out there, and you intuitively know you have the innate ability to create a new standard of life, then I believe that you and I can do this together. One step at a time. *Focused, Fit, and Fulfilled After 50!* is not a book designed to inundate you with more knowledge, or a simple "how-to" missive on the latest workout/diet combos. This is about lasting change and habits that will serve YOU and help you create a new destiny specific to your needs and unique desires. Knowledge is plentiful. Having a map to *applied knowledge* is where the real power reveals itself.

Why am I even qualified to write about these topics? Am I a scientist, doctor, nutritionist, or trained psychologist? None of the above actually. I'm just like you, someone that wants to do well and strives for meaning, looking for a better way. I believe I have finally cracked the code, for me at least, and the pages that follow are my absolute best efforts at sharing how I got there. I hope you will forgive the occasional rabbit hole or lost thread of an idea. If you are patient, I am optimistic you will find concepts that strike a nerve and lead you to your own epiphanies, your truth, and ultimately, to the top of your mountain. Are you ready to see new doors open for you too? I hope so! Let's do this together!

Section 1: FOCUS

"Where focus goes, energy flows." – Tony Robbins

I have long admired author, philanthropist, and crazy-cool life coach Tony Robbins. Volun-told by my boss in the early 1990s to go to one of Tony's four-day *Unleash the Power Within* seminars, I quickly became enamored with the clarity and adaptability of his messages. He just made good sense. So, I walked on hot coals, jumped up and down to every song, hugged perfect strangers, shifted my perspective, and promptly went home and changed my approach to life and work. I went from "happy to just get by" to a life and career filled with accolades and upward movement. As cliché as this may sound, that seminar changed my life. Tony shared so many powerful, life-affirming, results-oriented strategies that week, but the ones that hit me in my core, and created the greatest changes in my life, were all centered around the topic of focus. Boil it down to its most basic elements, Tony tells us that we make three core **decisions** in every moment. They are:

1. **What am I going to focus on?**

2. **What does this mean?**

3. **What am I going to do about it?**

For most of us, the answers to these questions are entirely within our ability to control. Where we focus our thoughts and energy is an ongoing personal choice, a decision we get to make every day, all day long. Unfortunately, many of us end up making these important choices based on the ingrained habits of our past, which is why we end up getting the same results, over and over again, despite our best intentions.

Renowned author, speaker, and neuroscientist Dr. Joe Dispenza describes the premise of habitual thoughts and repeated behaviors as *"Neurons that fire together, wire together."* He furthers the concept by sharing: *"As long as you are thinking equal to your environment, your personal reality is creating your personality and there is a dance between your inner world and the experience in the outer world..."*

What we choose to focus on, and the corresponding thoughts this attention generates, will either keep us anchored to the memories of our past or can propel us into that compelling future we have imagined. The direction is ours to choose. This also has everything to do with the level of success, fulfillment, joy, and inspired action we allow into our lives. We all have the same amount of time each day. Those who achieve their biggest, brightest dreams are those who turn the scattered ray of light that surrounds them into a laser beam of directed thought, aimed squarely at what they are attempting to accomplish. Simple, right?

I wish. My path to finding focus has been as long and winding as a highway through the Colorado mountains. Having traversed those passage-ways during several cross-country trips with Andrew and Nova, I can attest to the sense of wonder, connection, and appreciation you can feel one moment, followed quickly by moments of angst and hesitation, like when we drove through a snowstorm in the middle of the night with nowhere to pull off. During those white-knuckled moments we resolved to just stay calm and move forward, keeping faith that the next curve would bring clear visibility and a smoother experience. Sometimes that's still all I need to do today: remind myself to stay calm and keep moving forward.

Of course, "finding" focus assumes it is not only missing, but that once you discover it you are home-free, riding the ecstasy of connection from that moment on. In my experience it has been a journey that, yes, gets easier over time, but not a trip you ever finish. There will always be more roads to travel, more "states" to explore. I have joyously experienced pockets of arrival and achievement, but to finish searching would indicate I am no longer traveling, no longer striving for what's next. Personally, I know there will always be another goal, another story to write, a new map to explore.

What to Focus On?

My focus has certainly changed in the decades since that first Tony Robbins seminar. In my twenties it was all about social outings, time with friends, fitness, relationships, tournaments (I was an athlete, after all), and making enough money to fund all the above. In my thirties I became a mom, so focus shifted towards raising my son, family time, soccer games, and growing my career so I could still fund all the above. My forties presented more of the same at first, until I started to feel the unremitting pull of change again, an uneasiness that permeated my once peaceful routine. I eventually restarted an old relationship, made some substantial, if ill-advised, career moves, and bought a second home when the first one was fine. I even worked at sea onboard a cruise ship, which was awesome, but wreaked havoc on my home life. Mid-life crisis perhaps? Or the beginning of the end of the person I had grown to be during the first five decades on earth? I choose to believe it is the commencement of something beautiful. I think life beyond fifty, with the right amount of directed focus, is going to rock. I just needed the big goal so I could express this unlimited core of potential.

> *"If you are not being defined by a vision of the future, then you're left with the old memories of the past and you will be predictable in your life."*
> – Dr. Joe Dispenza on *Impact Theory* Podcast

The Power of <u>Your</u> Focus

In this section we are going to explore the deepest and most formidable topics presented in the book. We will dive into how to direct **Time** so that it serves you and doesn't hold you hostage to the past. I will share the most influential tool I have ever used, the art of **Pivoting**, while simultaneously showing you how to redirect negative thoughts and become a **BADASS**. We will then transition into the transcendental powers of **Meditation**, **Alignment**, and **Visualization**. Finally, we dig into why staying **Present** and releasing the need to **Multi-Task** is such a game-changer. These are the areas that will calibrate your laser and help you take aim at your own version of peak fitness and fulfillment.

Are you ready to feel the shift in your ability to direct your thoughts? Are you done with "the way it has always been"? Is now the time, finally, to dive headfirst into the compelling future you have always imagined? Great! Then off we go!

Time Is an Illusion

"People like us, who believe in physics, know that the distinction between past, present, and future is nothing more than a persistent, stubborn illusion."

– Albert Einstein

Einstein, the world's most recognizable name in science, famously stated, *"Time is an illusion."* When he shared this iconic assessment, he was ostensibly connecting the sentiment to the law of physics, relativity, and gravity. He illustrated the theory by asserting, *"When you are courting a nice girl an hour seems like a second. When you sit on a red-hot cinder a second seems like an hour. That's relativity."*

Theoretical Physicist Stephen Hawking took the principle a quantum leap forward, sharing his theory, *"Before 1915, Space and Time were thought of as a fixed arena in which events took place, but which was not affected by what happened in it. Space and time are now dynamic quantities. Space and time not only affect but are also affected by everything that happens in the Universe."* What do Einstein and Hawking have to do with our conversation about Focus and Time? *Everything.*

Both scientists suspected that our beliefs *relative to the dynamic of time* determined how time elapsed for us as individuals. For example, if we believe we can mold it, shape it, use it, stretch it out, and achieve more than previously believed possible, that is absolutely true! If, however, we hold as truth that the passage of time is beyond our comprehension of control, well, we would be correct there too. How does this play into achieving your dreams? Simple. If you believe that you do not have enough time to accomplish all that you want to achieve, you are right! Time will be your jailer, forever linking you to the past, making you susceptible to the whims of others and **their** beliefs on how you should spend your moments here on earth.

If, however, you recognize that how you utilize this precious resource is *entirely dependent on your choices* and the clarity of your vision, then this concept will set you on a course to reach the brightest suns in your personal universe, with far less effort than you may imagine! You will "affect," as Hawking declared, everything that happens in your world.

Putting it "Out There" and Manifesting Time

If you are spending a large portion of your day <u>escaping</u> from your life, mindlessly immersing yourself in the plethora of distractions available, then with some simple shifts you <u>will</u> have the time to pursue every single one of your goals. All of them. This chapter will help you make that change. Remember earlier when I shared that I had no idea how I was going to make this new adventure work for me? It's true, I personally questioned how I could possibly squeeze more time out of my already action packed, bell to bell, mentally exhausting day. As it turns out, time, or the lack thereof, really WAS an illusion for me.

In the months since I began exploring and probing this principle, I have freed up more of this precious resource than I even dreamed was possible. This allowed me to not only pursue personal best achievements in all three pillars (focus, fitness, and fulfillment), it also set me on a new and exciting course for a dynamic and soul-fulfilling future. If I can already harness my ability to stretch and mold time so early in this process, what else might I accomplish with practice? Imagine the possibilities! But first, to make the shift in earnest, I had to get real about where my time had been fundamentally, and pragmatically, going.

Exploring My "Daily Routine"

My first year in southern California passed by in the blink of an eye, and it wasn't because I was hanging out with celebrities and "California dreaming!" I was busy! Too hectic to think, or so I assumed. Have you ever heard people exclaim, *"I'm back to back all day, with barely enough time to catch a breath!"* or *"I'm working a ton right now. I'll relax more once we get through this quarter/project/client/fiscal year."* Yup, that was me. Life was too demanding to enjoy the fact that I lived in a beautiful state, surrounded by kind people, incredible restaurants, wineries, beaches, mountains, museums, golf courses, and cheesy "must see once" tourist attractions. And that's just scratching the surface! How does someone like me, who has the freedom and flexibility to determine how I spend my days, get "too busy" to enjoy life?

Simple. I got sucked into a vortex of predictable behavior that served the purpose of task completion, but did not serve my desire for expansion, growth, and fulfillment. I was the proverbial hamster on a wheel, burning all of my time and energy trying to keep things in motion. I was going somewhere for sure, but I couldn't tell you where, or even what the purpose was in getting there. Each day felt like an iteration of the day before, as well as a prophecy of the day to come. Does any part of this routine sound familiar?

- Wake up
- Caffeinate (green tea)

- Get back in bed, meditate for a few minutes, try to center
- Read the news, or at least the headlines
- Peek at social media and post a picture of Nova or how "awesome" yesterday was
- Get ready for work
- Drive to work listening to podcasts that inspire me
- Get to work, open email, immediately forgetting the lessons from the podcast
- Have more caffeine
- Back to email, work hard to do a good job (I like what I do, after all)
- Finish the day mentally exhausted, adrenals fatigued from caffeine and stress
- Drive home
- Make dinner
- Talk to the family
- Feed the dog
- Watch "just one" show on Netflix
- Decide I am too tired to think after 7 pm, watch a few more shows on Netflix
- Get up and turn everything off
- Take Nova out
- Get ready for bed

- Finally, go to bed and tell myself that *"starting tomorrow"* I'll do something different
- Get up the next day, rinse, repeat!

This routine was taking me nowhere but deeper into my fifties. At least I had the weekends to look forward to, right? When I first moved to California, weekends were an opportunity to explore this picturesque state, especially when Andrew visited (before he moved here too.). Even then my breakthrough moments were only short bursts of activity followed by a desire to get back to the comfortable, predictable routine. When I transitioned from the corporate apartment to a leased, expensive (California real estate prices are nuts) single family home, and Andrew and Nova joined me, I rarely ventured outside of my new, protective bubble. I had yardwork to do and "settling" to accomplish. In addition, since I was "too tired" to think at night my weekends became opportunities to study for the MBA, catch up on work email, and balance my checkbook, all while setting incredible goals about how I was going to change it all *someday*. Not exactly a "Focused, Fulfilled" life! Thank goodness I had family with me, as they created moments of joy every single day. I smile every time I look at the very expressive Nova, and Andrew is a reliable source of connection and pride.

With my seven-day week allegedly spoken for, I had to look for new and creative ways to really make a change. I also knew I would be required to decide what to change, eliminate, or repurpose if I was truly going to allow room for the "how" of my dream to reveal itself. It became obvious that the only way to create this shift was to dig a lot deeper into the routine referenced above. I had to review each effort, time commitment, and intended result, while matching it up against my big goals. I had to get real and take the blinders of comfort and predictability off for good. When I started this excavation, I unearthed a few shocking truths.

Freeing Up Time

The first a-ha realization was that I was burning time literally every morning and evening via my rituals. That cheerful little custom of green tea, news, and social media while still in bed would go on for well over an hour, sometimes even two. I am an early bird by nature and wake up between 4:30 and 5:00 am without an alarm, yet with this prolonged approach to "centering" before the day began, it would be 6:30 or 7:00 am before I actually had anything to show for my early morning exertions. I knew I had to find a way of making this time more effective.

In the evening, I was allowing myself to "believe" that I was not at my best at night, which made it easy to slip into the Netflix post-dinner coma and eliminate any potential constructive time there. Another hour or two completely wasted. As Henry Ford once shared, "*Whether you think you can, or you think you can't, you're right.*" I truly thought my brain didn't want to function at night, so I allowed the evening to be a playground for unproductive, time-wasting activities. When I finally invalidated this paradigm another pocket of time was freed up.

In addition, I started to discover that while I was always "busy" at work I was not always using my time in the most effective, results-oriented ways. How I spent my time was literally being dictated by Microsoft Outlook, and I was giving up my freedom to what was on my calendar and how many demands for my time and attention (aka emails) were in my inbox. *Outlook was running my life!* I bounced from meeting to meeting, blindly following the direction of calendar reminders and meeting invites that I rarely questioned. In between, I was furiously working my inbox, responding to all the questions that came my way. People needed me after all! Somehow it felt that if I could just "get it all done," even for a moment, I would achieve that seemingly unattainable sensation of accomplishment. As if a fleeting instant of having a clean inbox would somehow set things straight and make the world stand up and applaud. Outlook meant well, I'm sure, but I got to the point where I had to take control of my life again.

Of course, "taking control" came with a lot of internal incongruities between my brain and my soul. My brain was convinced it was always easier to start something BIG tomorrow after I got caught up. It can wait one more day! (More about the Tomorrow Syndrome later in the book. I had that one big time!) My soul, on the other hand, kept encouraging me to break out of this unproductive pattern of behavior and free up time for real expansion. I knew that I had to find a way to ensure the quality of my work was consistent, while directing my energy to the things that would make the biggest impact. Finding a way to achieve this was more important than simple task completion and a clean inbox.

> *"We think, mistakenly, that success is the result of the amount of time we put in at work, instead of the quality of time we put in."*
>
> – Arianna Huffington

Improved Approach to Time and Focus

As my epiphany generated goals were sinking deeper into my inner being, I realized beliefs about a "lack of time" would no longer be tolerated. The energy to create lasting change was already within me, and with this awareness ideas and energy began compounding rapidly. As a firm believer in the power of meditation (which I dedicate an entire chapter to) and journaling, I knew the first step was not to scientifically dissect every minute of my day. That would come. First, I had to **feel** what it would be like to have an abundance of time. I had to visualize experiencing a profusion of this resource, enabling me to complete a plethora of soul-satisfying goals. Then, and only then, would I move on to the analytical part of the equation, from the perspective of an aligned vision. *Feel first, analyze second.*

Using my aspiration of a home as the meditative thought starter, I took about thirty-minutes to focus on how, ultimately, it would feel to become the driver of my destiny and my time. I leaned into the sensation of having an abundance of energy and hours to complete all that I wanted to accomplish. I pictured making decisions that moved me towards my goals, and away from the task-centered, people-pleasing lifestyle that had once plagued me. As I completed this "feeling" exercise I sensed a dramatic shift in my energy and believed that I had all that I needed to make my dreams happen.

Once I was able to fully feel the abundance of time and energy enter my theoretical life, I explored some of those nagging, predictable time wasters listed above. With a little creative thought and a commitment to creating lasting changes, I quickly exposed areas that needed improvement. Here are some of the areas where I was able to free up time AND feel more energized in the process:

- **Early Morning**: I continue to wake up early, without an alarm, jazzed to begin another day. Now I give myself no more than a minute or two to transition from that state of "half asleep" to feet on the ground, ready to move. I include a quick moment of gratitude before I stand, saying something as swift as, *"Thank you, my soul, for that amazing sleep,"* or *"I'm going to love this day! Let's do this!"* Those bright sentiments prime my energy for a powerfully affirmative experience! Getting up and moving right away also reclaims the time that would have been spent in the in-between state of "almost awake" that truly serves no purpose.

- **Morning Routine**: I still wake up with green tea (Amazing Grass Green Superfood with Energy, Lemon Lime flavor, actually) and meditation, however, I have significantly decreased the amount of time I spend reading the news and catching up on social media. I grab a few news headlines, look at my notifications on social, and get on with it. This has produced well over an hour of additional productivity every day! Extrapolated out through an entire year, this one simple change has the potential to add over twenty-two full days of creativity back into my life! Twenty-two days (not counting sleep)! Additional time to write, design, stretch, exercise, or simply enjoy being alive and present. It has made a huge difference so far, including the ability to write a lot of the content for this book!

- **At Work**: Prioritization in the workplace is a skill needed to survive the demands of most jobs these days. For many of us there are usually more tasks to complete than there is time, so ordering your approach is often the difference between winning and losing, success and frustration. Looking deeply at how I arranged my efforts allowed me to completely rearrange how I tackled tasks like email and meetings. In addition, something as simple as being *fully present* was a game changer, eliminating the need to read the same email twice, or ask a peer to recap what they were just sharing. The ancillary benefit of persisting to stay present at all meetings allowed me to ascertain whether I was adding value by attending said gatherings. For those sessions where the answer was "no" or "only a little," I quickly opted out of future meetings, instead offering my attention if others had questions or needed follow up. This freed up hours of productive time each week and is an exercise I highly recommend.

- **Multi-Tasking**: Another belief I have woven through my approach to both work and my personal life is the fact that the brain cannot truly multi-task. It can quickly switch from one thing to the next; however, you cannot completely focus on two things at the same time. As an example, if you are in a meeting, and take a few seconds to read the important text message that popped up on your phone, or the email that dinged into your inbox, you are going to miss a few sentences of what was covered. A few sentences may not seem like much, because you are following the overall flow of the dialogue, however, when this is habitual, it can quickly derail any hopes of true productivity. I was able to get time back in my workday by *focusing on each task to the fullest.* You will be surprised how much this shifts your experience.

- **Evening Routine**: Like the lost time I was experiencing in the morning, I knew my weak-ass, senseless excuses about being too tired at night were not serving me well. I made one simple yet critical change: Instead of losing myself to that Netflix coma mentioned earlier, I now go into my home office after dinner and have a "power hour" of productivity every night. I dive into homework, a goal I am working on, work email, or getting more words on paper. I am often surprised how clear my brain really does think at night! If I do, occasionally, take a relaxing evening off to watch movies, it is because I chose to do so, not because it was demanded by my routine and lack of resourcefulness.

- **Social Media**: In general, this has never been a significant time suck for me, as I don't get a lot of joy over hours of scrolling on social. With that said, I respect this medium and those who use it to connect and share information. If time is an issue for you, though, you may want to do a gut check on how much time you spend on these sites. Also take note of how you _**feel**_ before, and after, a social media session. Are you uplifted and lighter? Or frustrated and angry at the posts you read that you didn't agree with? No matter what, this is still your time, so decide how much of it you choose to spend in this area.

After I completed my analysis, I discovered I had more than enough time to pursue the "big goals" that were knocking on the door. Once I shifted, I also found that I was happier nearly every day, more productive and aligned at work, and (as I may have mentioned) super jazzed about getting up in the morning! My daily foundation is now based on the fact that this is <u>my</u> time to spend, <u>my</u> energy to vibrate, and <u>my</u> life to create!

Freeing up time was the first necessary step to creating and achieving everything else in this book. My hope is that through these examples and simple exercises you too can create the space you need to generate lasting change too!

The Art of Pivoting, Perspective, and Being a Badass!

"Anytime you feel negative emotion, stop and say: Something is important here; otherwise, I would not be feeling this negative emotion. What is it that I want? And then simply turn your attention to what you do want...in the moment you turn your attention to what you want, the negative attraction will stop. And in the moment the negative attraction stops the positive attraction will begin. And – in that moment – your feeling will change from not feeling good to feeling good. That is the process of pivoting."

– Abraham-Hicks, Excerpted from the workshop
"Money and the Law of Attraction", August 31, 2008

The Power of Thought

You don't need to be a neuroscientist to realize that good thoughts feel good, and bad thoughts feel, well, you guessed it, bad. Try this quick experiment. Think of something pleasing that happened not that long ago. It could be as simple as making a slow-motion video of your dog that made you laugh, or a kind word that a co-worker said to you. Go there. See it. Live the moment again. How did that feel? Did you experience a similar feeling of joy or laughter welling up inside? Awesome! I still get goosebumps when I recall the memory of visiting the farm in Tennessee for the first time. Pure paradise! To this day that recollection produces a warmth around my heart that feels timeless.

Now, do the opposite, and bring forth a memory that upsets you. For this quick exercise please don't make it traumatic, any simple negative interaction will do. I can weirdly remember, vividly, a driver who cut me off one day, barely missing my front bumper and speeding off ahead. As is typical in congested central Florida traffic we met again at the next stop light. Human nature made me peer into the vehicle to see what a massive jerk really looked like, as if that would prove some internal point I was making. The driver never looked in my direction, but knew I was there, because he held up a pre-printed sign telling me the lyrical equivalent of raising both middle fingers. Then he drove off. I was shocked and infuriated and can *still* remember how it felt! Do you want to know the saddest part of the story? It happened twenty-seven years ago!

Our brains have the incredible ability to recall a wide variety of memories from our past in vivid detail, while completely burying others deemed less significant. (I wish I could bury the memory of that nasty driver)! With so many memories to choose from, why would we consciously decide to recall instances that do not generate a positive vibe?

The same principle holds true for what we decide to focus on. With so many options available for our mental consumption, why would we spend time and energy on topics that do not make us happy? A large part of this has to do with the chemical composition of our thoughts and an addiction to the way they feel. Dr. Joe Dispenza, who I introduced you to earlier, wrote a book called *"Breaking the Habit of Being Yourself."* It's a deep, provocative, and powerful manuscript, and I will not come close to imparting the essence of his key teaching points here in this paragraph, however, the spirit of it is this: When we think a thought, the brain releases chemicals that produce a corresponding feeling. When the thought is repeated, often the body begins to expect the biochemical response and we become addicted to the chemical signature of our very own thoughts, even when they do not serve us! Incredible! If you want to know more about this subject, I highly recommend reading any, or all, of Dr. Dispenza's books.

If negative thoughts are part of our hard-wired being how can we shift to a feeling that is more positive in nature? I believe this can be done through the art of "pivoting."

Pivoting

Look, I get it. I've been there too, held captive by dark, suffocating, swirling thoughts of regret or worry, some of which paralyzed my ability to act and move forward. It always started with one simple, negative thought, which innocently dumped the corresponding chemicals into my stomach. The slightly "off" contemplation called forth another matching memory or projection into the future, which created another, and another, and another. Next thing I knew I was either in a state of anxiety over perceived lack (of love, information, or context), or I was in a deep emotional slump, wondering when I would see the "light" of joy again. Pivoting proved to be what was missing in my life.

I first learned about this instrument when I attended a powerful Abraham-Hicks' seminar, conducted in Atlanta, GA on my 50th birthday. (A special shout out to my wonderful friend Jennifer for attending with me!) The energy there was remarkable, with Abraham speaking eloquently about the art of pivoting and the law of attraction! It was a memorable way to spend a milestone day. I have been utilizing this tool for a few years now, and the concept is fairly easy to explain. Simply said, pivoting is the ritual of curbing negative thinking in the ***early stages*** of thought while turning, or pivoting, to thoughts that feel better. Catching negative thinking in the early stages is key! Because our minds are searching for thoughts that are like the one before, this shift, or pivot, almost always puts us on a track to better feeling experiences and manifestations.

My son Andrew is an expert at pivoting. Years ago, he was fortunate enough to spend time with my good friend, and phenomenal mindset expert, Raffaella Russignaga of Kusala Consulting. After a few productive goal-setting sessions, I asked him what resonated the most in his chats with Raffy. *"The concept of pivoting,"* he quickly replied. *"It just makes so much sense!"* In the years since then he has nearly perfected this soul-saving, energy-protecting tool. He even helps me pivot when I come home in a slight funk or he can tell something is bothering me. This guy's a gem! I wished I had mastered this art when I was in my twenties!

> *"I play among the stars and then fall so low. I try to make sense as I go."*
>
> – Worlds Apart, Seven Lions featuring Kerli

Even the most positive, successful minds on the planet have succumbed to negative thoughts. It's going to happen. When you first find yourself mired in a painful rut of pessimism or defeat, it's hard to convince your brain to go all the way to joyful. The trick is shifting from negative contemplation to something that feels more neutral, and eventually to thoughts that make you feel good. How do you know when it is time to pivot? Do you really need to monitor every thought? Not at all. Just pay attention to how you feel. When you start to feel off, angry, annoyed, sad, impatient, scared, worried, or any other emotion that doesn't feel good, recognize where you are and get the hell out of there!

Be a BADASS!

It was while I was submerged in one such pocket of melancholy that I came up with an acronym that, to this day, helps me pivot out of almost any negative emotion, way before the slide is too deep. I wrote it in my journal back then and was able to recover it, nearly a year later, for the creation of this book. All I needed to do was become a **BADASS**. This is the entry I wrote to myself:

- **B**reathe in, breathe out, focusing on the sound and feel of your breath. (It is profound how this simple act has the power to slow the momentum of my thoughts. I think we forget to breathe when our heads are in chaos.)
- **A**cknowledge where you are. Recognize that you are in a swirl moment and call it what it is.
- **D**etermine where you *want* to be and *why*. How would you prefer to feel? What would you rather focus on in this moment?
- **A**ppreciate the ability to pause, that you can slow, stop, and redirect your thoughts. That's real power!
- **S**ee your future self. Visualize the best version of you, your happy and joyous story.
- **S**urrender to the positive flow! As good thoughts begin to stream in don't reject them with *logic*. "Yes, but…" will quickly reverse the flow of better feeling vibes. Don't let that happen.

This is the best pivoting tool I have ever experienced, and it has helped me avoid more pits of self-induced gloom than any other tactic I had tried previously or since. I'm not perfect, and I do still allow things to weigh on me from time to time, however, if I recognize the negative thought and catch the stream early enough, I can almost always turn it around. Shifting as soon as you recognize the angst, and before it gets too bad, can mean the difference between whipping yourself into a frenzy and texting your ex in the middle of the night, and slowly realizing that you are safe, whole, and worth all sorts of joy and happiness. Or between worrying yourself sick over the possibility of a catastrophic event and choosing to focus on the good that surrounds you right now. Deal with the bad if it comes.

> *"A coward dies a thousand deaths, a brave man only once."*
>
> – Confucius

Sometimes the Universe Helps Us Out

As much as I have learned and practiced the art of pivoting, I still can work myself into a pocket of negative, unproductive thoughts. On those days I can sense myself operating with a short fuse, loads of impatience, and a lack of self-discipline. When I am in this mode, if I do not pivot on my own, I can usually count on something to interrupt my pattern and nudge me back into alignment.

The most recent example was on a Saturday afternoon when I was pressing, really pushing, to get things done. I completely forgot to mentally rest and find moments of "presence" on my day off, getting sucked once again into that mindset of "I've got shit to do!" The interruption came by way of an emergency with my sweet girl, Nova. As I was exercising in the garage, while simultaneously doing laundry and straightening up our "home gym," I walked outside to see Nova chewing a tennis ball. I didn't give it much thought until I went back ten minutes later and noticed that half of the ball was completely gone! I checked the grass and surrounding area and knew within seconds that there was only one other possibility. Nova had swallowed half of a tennis ball! What I didn't know was that if she had ingested large pieces that could block her intestines or smaller bits that had a decent chance of passing. I called the emergency vet and they suggested I come in. Crap. I loaded Nova in the car and headed for a visit that I knew would be both expensive and time consuming, interrupting my intended flow of compulsory productivity.

I sat in the waiting room of a perfectly pleasant practice, clearly emitting a "*don't talk to me unless you have to*" vibe. Nova, on the other hand, thought it was an exciting outing and wanted to be friends with everyone, wagging her tail and straining for sniffs with every dog that entered. I remembered feeling annoyed as I sat there, but not the least bit worried. The vet tech eventually came to take Nova back, asking that I stay in the waiting room. The tech also causally mentioned the word "surgery," as in, "if we can't make her vomit it up, we may need to do surgery, but we are hoping to avoid that." *Wait, what?* That got my attention and clearly interrupted my self-induced, inward-focused state.

The next fifteen minutes seemed significantly longer (remember Einstein and relativity?), as I stewed on every sentiment from *"how could she eat the ball"* to *"how could I allow her to eat that POS ball!"* Eventually, the tech brought me back and introduced me to the veterinarian. I was fully present then! He shared the good news that they were able to get most of the rubber out through vomiting, and x-rays showed no large pieces remaining. The tears started to well in my eyes as I thanked him profusely for taking care of my girl. The tech then brought me my sweet dog, who looked at me like we had been separated for a week. Her eyes clearly said, "Mom! That wasn't fun at all!" as she leapt into my arms and kissed my hands with alacrity. I checked out, paid, and took Nova to the car where I promptly began to sob. Whatever had been building up released. I knew in that moment that I had been pushing too hard, trying to force results, and the abrupt and unintended break allowed me to stop the momentum.

Pivoting in Action

Pivoting our thoughts applies to far more than just turning negative thoughts into positive ones. This tool can also help us avoid damaging internal dialogue that could derail the best of our intentions, as well as our most fervent dreams. I vividly remember a time, several years ago, where I utilized pivoting to help me reverse a potentially self-defeating mindset that was about to talk me out of pursing something wonderful.

When I was in my mid-forties, I left a stable, well-paying job of fifteen years to move to the horse farm in the mountains that I mentioned earlier. I was in pursuit, as always, of a simpler life and a new beginning that would help me find my elusive center. With the work experience I had accumulated, mostly as a leader within a Fortune 100 company, I was able to quickly land a job in my new town.

Unfortunately, the leaders I went to work for ran the business on the shady side, a trait I had not experienced in my former workplace. Still, even with the misalignment in ethics I truly believed the answer was simple. *Put more effort into it! Work harder! You can still do it the right way!* Yet, the harder I worked the farther away from joy, satisfaction, and abundance I seemed to get.

Eventually, I found a part-time role to supplement the first job, and for almost a year poured all of my energy into making both jobs work to get me back to a place of stability. I continued to believe that *more effort meant better results*, yet, I had a negative balance in my personal satisfaction levels and was becoming more and more dejected each day. I knew I deserved more and began to seek out answers to the questions that were plaguing me. *Why is this so difficult? Why am I not realizing results when I am working seven days a week? How can I make these jobs bring me a sense of satisfaction and results?* I was incredibly unhappy and always exhausted. I had to find a way to pivot out of this situation and make it better.

An Opportunity to Change

Eventually I found a job as an officer on a cruise ship that allowed me to leave that disaster of a business, however, ultimately the new position wasn't a long term solve either. It included very long pockets of time away from my family and the farm that I loved so much. I know this going in, but the impact on my homelife was much steeper than I had anticipated.

After two years at sea, I knew it was time to return to land. My family unit was falling apart and the sustained absences were not advocating for any semblance of a balanced life. One day, I was causally searching a job site and I tripped upon an available opportunity within the company I had left to move to the farm. The role was amazing, and the requirements matched my experience perfectly. I read every detail of the job description repeatedly, working on "feeling" each and every line. Excitement coursed through my veins as I began to visualize getting the role and working for this well-respected company again!

Within moments, however, familiar doubts began to creep in: *Maybe I'm not good enough. Am I smart enough to contribute to a company full of powerful people? I will be leading a seasoned team of business leaders. Do I have enough to offer experienced managers for this leading-edge corporation?*

Hesitation weaved its way through my psyche to the point that I started to doubt that I should even apply for the position. My brain casually reminded me, "*Things are not **that bad** right now.*

Maybe you should just stay where you are." That made sense! "*After all,*" my mind continued, "*you really like the people you work with, and being at sea is kind of a cool lifestyle!*" Have you ever done that? Talked yourself out of a good idea by convincing yourself that the *known* was a far safer option, and not all that bad?

Thank goodness I slept on it and woke up in a better state, remembering that I had all that I needed, within myself, to be successful. I knew, without a doubt, that I was an experienced and successful leader and that I had a lot to offer. As I felt joy flowing through me, I read the job description again. This time I felt "*Yes! This job was meant for me!*" Without hesitation I started the online application and confidently posted an updated copy of my resume. By the time I hit send I already *knew* I had the job.

A week later, I received a phone call to set up the initial interview, and four interviews later I was sitting in front of my future peers as my new leader asked if I wanted to join the team. My answer was an immediate "*yes!*" I remember feeling both immense gratitude and excitement for what was to come. I recall how appreciative I was for my ability to redirect my self-defeating inner dialogue and turn it into something that would propel me forward. A good skill to have indeed!

Perspective

*"When you change the way you look at things, the
things you look at change."*

– Dr. Wayne W. Dyer

Perspective, like pivoting, is a powerful, life affirming tool.
It is also one that is not used enough these days, as much of our
interaction (especially online), has been rendered into quick sound
bites and headlines intended to get you to click on the link or react.
Personally, I am working on not buying into the hype,
remembering that there is always more to the story, and an
individual's feelings about a topic may be different depending on
their perspective going in. The movie, *Vantage Point*, with Dennis
Quaid, illustrates this concept perfectly. A scene is introduced at
the beginning of the movie and is then played repeatedly
throughout the film, each time through the view, or perspective, of
a different person. Fascinating! While people often say that truth
is truth, I still believe that your perspective can absolutely shape
how you feel about a situation.

My mom was a nurse for over forty years. Growing up, and
even later in life when I visited her faithfully every summer with
Andrew, I never recall her complaining about life in the hospital.
Sometimes she would say she was a bit tired if her shifts were long,
but her outlook was that she was where she was supposed to be,
and the appreciation for her nursing experiences emanated from

her being. Instead of negativity, I remember her sharing praise for the great leaders and friends she worked alongside, such as her long-time boss Vicky, and her wonderful friend Rona, who is still her BFF today. For my mom it was simply a matter of perspective.

I recall the time she was featured in an article in the *Democrat and Chronicle*, Rochester New York's local paper. There was a beautiful picture of my mom assisting a patient right there on the front page, "above the fold," as they say in the newspaper business. While the article focused on the enduring issue of cutbacks in the nursing ranks, my mom kept an optimistic and patient-centered outlook on it all. "*I know I can walk into a room and make a difference in that person's day.*" That's how I remember my now-retired mom in the role she was meant for.

Perspective Examples

Still believe that a situation cannot have two different meanings? Look at the following illustrations and see if they shift your perspective on, well, perspective:

Illustration #1: Two nurses from Western Regional Hospital have just arrived at their respective homes and are about to share the highlights of the day with their spouses. Which nurse is more aligned?

Nurse #1:

Spouse: How was your day, honey?

Nurse 1: Well, Charlene called in again today. I swear she calls in every time there's a school holiday. I don't know why THEY won't do anything about it. It's so obvious. Mona was in her usual foul mood and said something snippy to me at lunch. I don't even remember what it was, but it ruined my afternoon.

Spouse: I'm sorry to hear that, dear.

Nurse 1: It doesn't matter. Just another typical shift at Western. I was on my feet most of the day because we were short staffed, and no one even seemed to notice or care. So much for the work-life balance they keep promising us. And you know what? The patient's families are getting ruder by the moment too! What's up with people these days? This one guy was abrupt with me when I went to check on his wife. He asked me the same question three times in a row. I kept telling him I didn't know when the doctor would be in to see them. Like I have any control over those prima donnas. Oh, well. Not like I can do anything about it. Sometimes this job is such a waste of my time. Whatever. Maybe *I'll* call in sick tomorrow. Let someone else carry the load for a while.

Nurse #2:

Spouse: How was your day, honey?

Nurse 2: Today was beautiful, my love. Boy, it went by fast, too! Charlene called in today, so Ann and I covered her patients. Poor dear. She's been working so hard to find trustworthy day care for her autistic son. Every time there's a school holiday she gets in a bind. I feel so bad for her, because I know she's trying. I'm going to talk to Fernando tomorrow, see if he has any recommendations. The leaders have been patient with her too, which is refreshing to see.

Spouse: You're sweet, honey. I'll ask around, too.

Nurse 2: Thank you, baby. Mona seemed a little stressed today, but after lunch we walked outside for a minute and she seemed to relax a little. I know she's caring for her elderly mom right now and has had some tough decisions to make.

Spouse: That's a heavy load. I hope she can work it out.

Nurse 2: She will. Mona has a heart of gold. Oh, and honey, let me tell you a quick story. I walked into Stella's room this afternoon, you know, the sweet woman that's recovering from a stroke. Well, her husband was there just as he always is, but this time he looked so worried. He had been waiting for the doctor all morning to get his wife's test results and they had not arrived yet. He shared with me that he had asked a few of the other nurses but no one seemed willing to find out. Even though I was already stretched thin, I went to the desk and made a few phone calls. I was finally able to reach the attending physician's office and they paged the doctor immediately, who said he was on his way. When I shared this with Stella's husband he started to cry! The look of relief and gratitude in his eyes, oh honey, that's why I decided to become a nurse! Moments like that!

It's easy to spot alignment and a positive perspective, right!? Let's look at one more example, this time from the world of sales:

Michelle Baker

Illustration #2:

Scenario: Two sales professionals who work for the same company are at the annual conference, networking with peers at opposite ends of the convention center. Who is more aligned?

<u>**Salesperson #1:**</u>

Jim (Trade show participant): Hey there! Haven't seen you in a while! How's it going?

Sales Pro 1: Jim! (Shaking hands firmly) So nice to see you again! It's been a banner year, my friend. Living the dream!

Jim: Wow, that's fantastic! So, what's up? Did you make record sales this year or something? Last time we met you were considering leaving the company. In fact, I distinctly remember you complaining about how lousy the managers were, and something about the impossible goals they kept assigning everyone.

Sales Pro 1: (Blushing slightly) Yes, I remember that chat vividly.

Jim: What happened? You get a new leadership team or something?

Sales Pro 1: Nope. Same group, and even higher sales targets! I had some tough decisions to make, Jim. It eventually led to a little, well, let's just call it soul searching, and I discovered that *I* was the real problem, not the leadership team. Most days I came to work already defeated and making excuses before I even started. That's easy to do in the business we are in! At that time every prospect I encountered was just another opportunity to be rejected, insulted, or flat out ignored. After a while I could feel the "no" before the real dialog had even begun!

Jim: Well, that's not exactly a recipe for success. How'd you turn it around?

Sales Pro 1: A new mindset! At the end of the day, I realized that I really love this company and believe in the product. I spent a solid month analyzing my approach and found some ugliness in the way I was thinking. I got rid of the bad habits, read books that helped me center, and pretty much re-engineered who I was as a salesperson. I can already feel the shift, and if this last quarter is any indication it is going to be a year to remember!

Jim: Hey, well done!

Sales Pro 1: Thank you, Jim! Listen, gotta run. The keynote starts in five minutes and I heard this speaker is amazing. Talk soon!

Salesperson #2:

Carolina (Trade Show participant): Well, hello there! How are things going? You made the convention again, so it must be looking pretty good for you!

Sales Pro 2: Oh, I've had better years.

Carolina: What's going on?

Sales Pro 2: People just don't get it anymore. The market is so diluted with garbage, and even when you have a strong online presence, they still buy the product that's cheaper. It's hard to reach people because the leads are a joke, and when I do get through to a real buyer, they either don't have time, or they want me to slash my prices to the point where the margin is crap. If I had a nickel for every fool that said no to me, well, I guess I wouldn't have to sell this junk anymore, now would I?

Carolina: Wow. That's heavy. Well, at least you are here! The leaders must still believe in you!

Sales Pro 2: Our leadership team is a joke. They think they know how to run a business and inspire the salesforce but, I'm telling you, they couldn't sell ice in the desert. What could they possibly teach me? I'm over it.

Carolina: Sure sounds like it. Hey, maybe you'll get some fresh ideas here at the conference. Have you been to see any of the keynote speakers this week?

Sales Pro 2: Are you kidding me? A bunch of over-inflated egos if you ask me. They just want to promote their books and get another speaking gig. Not for me. You go right ahead. I plan on beating the crowd to the bar.

Have you ever taken a good look at how you perceive things? Where are you on the spectrum of positivity? Can you relate to the complaining nurse or the joyful one? The optimistic sales rep or the one filled with excuses? Are those closest to you at work negative and filled with conspiracy theories, or enthusiastic and filled with gratitude? Who are you aligning with, and why? Remember, no matter where you work there is good and bad to be found in any situation. Except for outright harassment, most environments are not hostile in nature. What type of person, situation, conversation, and vibration are you attracting?

Conclusion on Pivoting and Perspective

As I mentioned towards the beginning of this chapter, discovering the art of pivoting was one of the most useful tools I have learned in my lifetime. There will always be good things to focus on, and the potential for bad as well. How I have chosen to answer those initial questions posed by Tony Robbins, *"What am I going to focus on?"*; *"What does this mean?"*; and *"What am I going to do about it?"* have helped me in more ways than I can name. I suggest you try the same, striving for that positive perspective that you know is inside of you. And remember, if all else fails, just be a BADASS!!!

Meditation and Aligning With the Best Version of You!

I own the most magnificent valley in the entire universe. It is so beautiful that I immediately feel a deep sense of peace every time I visit. There is a glorious, curving creek with crystal clear water that runs through the middle of my valley. The only sound you will ever hear is the bubbling flow of the water and the gentle breeze softly rustling the tall pines that grow on three sides. Occasionally, you will see deer quietly nibble along the edges of the dell, and I can't say I blame them for hanging out, for there is no threat of predators in this place. The grass is incredibly soft and inviting, so no shoes are required or even encouraged. Two comfortable Adirondack chairs sit right on the edge of the meadow, facing the creek, encouraging you to sit and rest for a spell, which I often do, sometimes mentally working through things that are tormenting me. I always find a way to sort them out here in this tranquil habitat. The air is always pleasantly warm, and did I mention it never rains in my valley? This is, by far, the most peaceful place in existence. For me, and me alone. Where is this magical place?

It's All in Your Head

As you may have guessed, this always sunny, perfectly peaceful valley resides within my imagination. In my world this location is as real as the house I sit in today, or the farm in Tennessee I used to go home to. This wonderful space has helped me work through so many situations that would have plagued me otherwise. It even got me through two hours of dental work with nothing to help except Novocain. I literally spent that entire dental procedure in the valley, feeling the sun on my face instead of the dentist's operating light, hearing the wind and the creek instead of the drilling and water splashing. I believe both the dentist and his tech were surprised at how calm I was. At one point she asked me if I needed to take a break, and I mumbled "Nah, I'm good!" Love. My. Valley.

The Power of Meditation

Why is a story about a place that exists only in my mind relevant to the topic of focus? Because I believe that there is power in the ability to close your eyes and center, blocking out the noise and distractions that are ever present in our lives. It is a peaceful, sunny, quiet valley for me (with a horse stable on just the other side of the pine trees, by the way). It may be a beach, the top of a mountain, drifting though outer space, or even just a feeling of quiet nothingness for you. For me, the best way to get there is through meditation.

Meditation is a simple exercise, and like any other skill, the more you practice the better you get. Meditation has a number of relevant benefits, such as starting the day in a positive way, quieting the mind when it wants to run wild, or helping you achieve a more peaceful state so you can center and prepare for what's next.

There are as many ways to practice meditation as there are olives on a tree in California's Central Valley. They all have the potential to provide the mindfulness that the practitioner is seeking, so it's important that you discover a method that works well for you. There are even apps that can take you through the basics! ("Headspace" is one that I have tried. It's very good!) If you do not currently practice any form of meditation, and would like to try, here's the practice that works well for me:

1. **Find a Quiet Space**: I can meditate practically anywhere, for any length of time. I have even caught a quick mindset break at a red light while driving. With that said, my recommendation is to start your meditation practice by finding a quiet place where you will be free of interruption. I am not partial to light versus dark, or dark over light. It's all about centering your mind, and to be able to do that day or night is a wonderful gift.

2. **Your Body**: Sit in a comfortable position where you can relax your shoulders while allowing your head, neck, legs, knees, and spine to relax into a neutral position. A soft chair where your back is supported and you can sit up straight, with your knees resting comfortably at a 90-degree angle, feet flat on the floor, is ideal. You can also try sitting on a pillow on the floor, legs crossed under or stretched out in front of you, with your back resting against another pillow placed against the wall. The notion here is that your body is comfortable without being completely prone. Are you comfy? Good. Let's begin!

3. **Your Breath**: With eyes still open take ten deep breaths, in through the nose, out through the mouth. On the third breath gently close your eyes, continuing to breath in and out. In through the nose, out through the mouth, focusing

on the sound of your breath, the sensation of the air flowing through you. Asking your brain to focus on something as immediate as the sound of your breath is a great way to begin the shift to relaxation. On the eighth breath, close your mouth and simply breathe through your nose in a comfortable rhythm. Continue to focus on the sound and sensation of your breath, but this time add two statements, said in the quiet and comfort of your own mind: "*Right now there's nowhere else to be, there's nothing else to do. There's nowhere else to be, there's nothing else to do.*" Say this a few more times then watch the words dissolve in your mind, seeping into your being. "*There's nowhere else to be, there's nothing else to do.*" Breathe in, breathe out.

4. **Body Scan**: By now you are probably feeling more tranquil. This is a wonderful time to do a top to bottom, or bottom to top, body scan. Personally, I like to start with my toes and slowly work my way up to the crown of my head. I focus on my toes, eyes still closed, and simply invite them to relax. I picture my toes easing into a perfect state of quiet relaxation. Then I move on to my feet, feeling them release all the built up stress or fatigue from walking and supporting my body. I usually send each body part some gratitude as I go, and in the case of my feet I may say "*Thank you, feet, for keeping me balanced and moving all day long. You are amazing.*" Then, it's on to my ankles, calves, knees, etc. until I get to the top of my head. Each

section takes only three or four slow breaths. By the time you get to the top (or the bottom), you should feel completely relaxed.

5. **Your Thoughts**: Now that you are relaxed, still focused on your peaceful, steady breathing, you may feel your thoughts slowing down a bit. Don't worry if unwanted, busy thoughts sneak back in. That's completely normal. Recognize the thought, send it some love (regardless if it is a good thought or a bad one), then shift your focus back to the sound and sensation of your breath. Breathe in, breathe out. Over time, you will notice that fewer pesky thoughts are sliding in, demanding to be acknowledged. This is the part of meditation I adore, as it is always fascinating to see what thoughts make their way into my now relaxed and peaceful mind. A mind that is unobstructed by the body's need for attention.

6. **Gratitude 2+1:** Once your body is relaxed, it is time to transition to a more directed part of the meditation, and it all starts with gratitude. Eyes still closed, body now completely relaxed, or at least more relaxed then when you began, pick two things you are grateful for. Express why it is they make you feel this appreciation. I don't pre-select who or what I am grateful for, as I am always curious to see what bubbles up. My son Andrew, Nova, some of my dearest friends, and my family are frequent flyers in this space. But sometimes I am surprised as I conjure a thought

of appreciation for my amazing chiropractor Jason, or the wonderful woman at work, Pavi, who always gives me a hug and asks about Andrew when I see her. *"Namaste Ji"* we share in greeting! Finding two things to appreciate is usually not a difficult task, especially when you are as calm and centered as you are now. After you feel gratitude for two external things, events, or people, come up with one thing you appreciate about yourself. Sometimes it is as simple as your ability to "stay the course" or "be kind". On other occasions it can be more specific. Gratitude 2+1 has the propensity to place you in a state of even deeper peace and serenity.

7. **Meditation with Mantras**: Finally, it's time to utilize this sense of peace to further direct your thoughts to vibrations that will serve your well-being and stated goals. I call this section "meditation with mantras" because it is a beautiful place to insert sentiments that you would like to weave into the fabric of your being, or at least your day! Once you are through the 2+1 gratitude practice, simply shift your thinking to a few statements that you will repeat ten to fifteen times each. In this case, it is okay to do a little pre-planning, having two to three statements lined up. If you don't remember them when you are in a meditative state don't worry, either move on to the next one or make up something fresh. Continue to breathe and say each sentence

slowly, ten to fifteen times, trying to feel the emotion of each line.

Examples of powerful mantras include:

    a. My beautiful body is fit, clean, and energized!
    b. My mind is clear and ready to generate aligned thoughts!
    c. My soul is grateful for the journey, the love, the potential!
    d. I love and am loved.
    e. I am a happy and joy-filled leader.
    f. Every day I am getting stronger!
    g. I have so much peace in my life!

When you are done with your mantras, spend a few minutes to recognize what comes up. It could be an idea, an emotion, or even a sense of peace you have never felt before. Take mental note of it. Lean into it. Then send it a layer of appreciation. Cool, right? Finally, take a few deep breaths and slowly open your eyes. It's important to take stock of how you feel in the moment when you are done, while listening carefully for any additional aligned thoughts or ideas that might be generating. I keep my journal close to me during meditation in case something does present itself. (I am pretty sure that is where BADASS came from.) Remember, meditation is not about completely stopping thoughts, so don't pressure yourself, or feel that the meditation has failed if you couldn't get your uninvited, nagging thoughts to stop. They will in time. Be kind to yourself and keep at it.

Once I significantly improved my ability to center and focus through daily meditation, I found it a lot easier to save my energy for things that really mattered, like my massive, compelling goals! It was time to use this extra vitality to pursue that which mattered most.

Imagination and Visualization

"It's the possibility of having a dream come true that makes life interesting."
> – The Alchemist by Paulo Coehlo

Philosophers have been telling us for years that everything we achieve starts as a simple thought. A thought becomes a desire, a desire begets a dream. Once we have a dream in place, and we believe in our ability to achieve it, the rest, as they say, is history. To make this happen, however, you need both ends of that stick: The desire AND the belief to achieve it.

Our old friend Einstein was an amazing scientist, of course, yet he was as much a philosopher as he was pragmatic and analytical. Best known for his equations (E=MC2 anyone?) and his 1921 Nobel Prize in Physics, Einstein was also a dreamer. My favorite Einstein quote resonates well with this topic of visualization.

*"**Imagination** is more important than knowledge."*
> – Albert Einstein

Nineteenth-century writer and philosopher Henry David Thoreau, author of "Walden" and many other missives, also recognized the power of imagination and goal setting, sharing:

> *"If one advances confidently in the direction of his dreams, and endeavors to live the life which he has **imagined**, he will meet with a success unexpected in common hours."*
>
> – Henry David Thoreau

These wise mentors knew the importance of the mind/manifestation connection, and the innate power of a vision that encourages you to move forward! And we all know it too, intuitively. There is nothing more satisfying than a journey towards a goal that you believe in. As I continued to explore the benefits of improved focus, I also discovered the criticality of aligning with a vision that is so real I can already feel the physical manifestation of it in my life. Remember, a step taken towards a goal is always more joyous than standing still.

I have been a master of imagination my entire life, though few would have called it that in my early years. *"Day Dreamer?"* Sure. *"Introvert?"* Probably. *"Shy and aloof?"* All day long. Little did they know that I was dreaming immense reveries, seeing myself play a starring role in all sorts of heroic adventures. In truth, I wanted to be anywhere but where I was, the reticent new girl in every classroom. Most days, I would pay attention for a little while, mostly out of fear that the teacher would suddenly call on me. The appeal of another world had a stronger pull on my attention, however, and it wasn't long before I detached myself from reality and plunged into my daydreams again.

"Make yourself the hero of your own movie!"

– Joe Rogan

It wasn't just the escapism that was alluring. I have always felt there was something special buried deep, and I mean deep, inside of me. Something that promised more than I was, beyond what my predictable path seemed to indicate was even possible. Mentally escaping always brought me closer to this inner being that seemed to know all about the potential that I had. This possibility of a new, exciting, expansive life was all the fuel I needed to break the bonds of my less than ideal surroundings and mentally transport myself into these dreamlike realms. To this day, at well over fifty years old, I still feel the pool of potential that radiates from within.

If daydreaming was an affliction, then I had it bad. I vividly remember a time in grade school when we were learning to write letters in cursive. Do you recall those sheets of paper where you wrote the letter "a" in cursive, like fifty times, practicing your curves and lines over and over again? I do. I would always get the first two or three lines completed, industriously focused on making the cleanest cursive letters possible. Within minutes, without fail, my mind began to drift, and my eyes slowly shifted to the trees seen through my classroom window. A simple thought like, *I wonder what Sahara (my horse) is doing right now* would send me off on a fifteen-minute adventure: Sahara and I racing through the fields to save my younger brother, who was my best friend at the time, from some unknown danger. We always saved the day, of course, and then Mike and I would build a campfire and regale each other with our stories of heroism.

My visions were always shattered by the sound of the teacher's voice calling *"Two minutes."* Oh shit! Pencil still in hand, I rapidly started writing "a, a, a, a, a, a, a" in the ugliest cursive you can imagine, turning in my work right under the wire. In reflection, it's a small wonder I even made it into middle school. I couldn't help it, though, I was a dreamer, and I still have big aspirations. My handwriting, however, never recovered and still looks like crap.

The Power of Visualization?

Visualization, according to Dictionary.com, is a *"technique involving focusing on positive mental images in order to achieve a particular goal."* Wikipedia explains that it is the *"cognitive process of purposefully generating visual mental imagery, simulating or recreating visual perception in order to maintain, inspect, or transform those images, consequently modifying their associated emotions or feelings."* In a nutshell, this means we have the ability to create images in our own minds with profound clarity, and once we do, we can shape these images, change them, and enhance them until they look and feel exactly as we want them to be!

The brain is the most amazing, and arguably the most malleable, organ in the body. Besides controlling bodily functions, storing our memories, and serving as the command center for the nervous system, the brain also holds an integral piece of the manifestation puzzle. Your beautiful mind contains trillions of synapses, all capable of converting electrical signals (thoughts) into their chemical equivalents (responses), and vice versa. The brain is so skilled at generating thoughts and chemical responses *that the body cannot differentiate between a real and an imagined event.* Welcome to the world of visualization!

Visualization is when you intentionally experience an event in advance and mold it to your desired outcome. It's when you close your eyes (in most cases) and mentally rehearse a scene exactly as you want it to be, perfecting it as you go. For example, if you are a decent golfer, but struggle with putting, you may visualize a smooth stroke and the ball going into the cup every time! If you struggle giving presentations in front of groups, you can visualize a flawless delivery, with participants nodding in agreement as you speak! Many have used visualization to become better leaders, musicians, interviewees, horseback riders, runners, sprinters, soccer players, chefs, etc. There really is no limit to how this can be used.

Visualization is being utilized in the world of sports with an ever-increasing degree of sophistication. Many athletes use this practice as an integral part of their structured training plan, allocating time each week to mentally simulating aspects of competition repeatedly in high levels of detail. The more they can feel, see, and hear the event during the visualization exercise, the more it helps with their overall training efforts. Another bonus of visualization for an athlete; – you can "train" just about anywhere, at any time! No equipment, stadium, or snow required. Just you and your imagination.

When this is a mastered skill, an individual can not only see the event, they can and often do <u>feel</u> what is taking place in the scenario. This, in part, is because when we visualize an action we stimulate the same synapses in the brain that activate when we are physically performing the activity. Do this repeatedly, with intent, and the brain will begin to wire in different ways, creating new paths and memories of events that may or may not have previously occurred in 4D physicality. Have you ever felt your arm jerk up because you were dreaming about something being thrown your way? Ever run in your sleep and wake up with your legs still twitching? Nova does this all the time, all four paws moving in unison as she gleefully, I imagine, gets close to that squirrel that has been teasing her from the tree in our back yard.

The first time I heard anyone mention "visualization" was in relation to an Olympic athlete and their training program. I don't remember who, what year, or the specific event it was, though I do know it was related to track and field. I recollect reading about how they would conduct the event, moment by moment, step by step, repeatedly in their head, and that doing so made the actual races almost effortless. As an athlete myself, I remember thinking "Whoa. That's powerful!" After that, I would practice turning double plays in my head (I was a shortstop), seeing the fluidity of motion, feeling the perfect pivot, delivering a bullet to first base, beating the runner by a step every time. I loved it!

Michael Jordan, one of my favorite athletes growing up (so much so that my son's middle name is "Jordan"), used to visualize successfully taking the winning shot of every game. He wanted the ball in his hands at that critical moment because he had already seen himself making the shot thousands of times in his mind. It was almost inevitable that he would make it in real life too!

Practice Visualizing

A simple illustration of this premise is as follows: Imagine yourself walking to your refrigerator. Can you see it in front of you? What color is it? Does your refrigerator have two doors or just one? Now open the door. There, on the shelf immediately in front of you, is a nice yellow lemon. (Organic or non, your choice. And pay no attention to your brain if it is arguing with you about whether or not you might actually have a lemon in the refrigerator right now.)

Take this beautiful lemon to the counter, grab the nearest sharp knife and a cutting board, and slice the fruit into quarters, watching the juice spill onto the board as you go. Now hold one quarter of the lemon up and deeply inhale its fresh, clean lemony scent. It's no wonder they use lemon in many cleaning products! Now, open your mouth and take a big bite out of the center of the fruit! Let the juice roll over your tongue and chew on the pulp a little.

Did your mouth water?

You knew intuitively you were simply reading words on a page, yet your body responded as if it were about to bite into a juicy lemon. (Your mouth is probably STILL watering!) That is visualization in action. If you can convince your brain that it is about to bite a lemon with only a small amount of effort, imagine what you can accomplish with focused intent.

What would it physically feel like to achieve the goal you are thinking about? For the job seeker, it might be the vision of walking into a room with confidence and peace, knowing that interviewing is something they are good at. For the out of shape mom, it might be seeing herself following through with her fitness goals, watching the glow emanate from her body in a state of peak energy. For the bowler it could be calmly walking to the lane and feeling the confidence of knowing all ten pins are going to fall. For me, and my dream of the farm, it is the simple moments I visualize. Like greeting my mom in the foyer of my dream home and inviting her in to hang up her coat and have some coffee. Or walking down the long and winding driveway to do morning chores, Nova dutifully by my side. I have been there so many times that it is sometimes a surprise when I open my eyes and remember that the kitchen is not yet mine (as of the writing of this book at least), and the chores will have to wait.

So how does it work? How exactly do you visualize?

Well, to begin with, you already do it! Every day! When you can mentally see the events of your experience in advance you can visualize. When you stress and worry about the pain you might feel while sitting in the dentist's chair three days from now, or you are stressing about a speech you must give this afternoon, feeling the words jumble up in your throat, you are visualizing. What I am focusing on here, however, is the practice of purposeful, goal-specific, *positive outcome* visualization. The steps are quite simple, and like anything else, the more you practice the better you will get.

To understand the process of purposeful, positive outcome visualization, I suggest you practice with something specific, like a job interview, walking around your dream home, or looking in the mirror and seeing the fit version of you staring back.

Visualization Practice

1. **Relax**: The first step in visualization, like meditation, is to relax. Find a quiet room and turn off your mobile devices for a few minutes. (You are so worth it!) Sit

quietly and focus on calming each part of your body. As you focus on each segment ("hello feet"), see the body part relaxing, taking a little break from the world, and sliding into the simplicity of just being. Listen to your breath, but don't try to control it. Let it flow. In and out. Out and in.

2. **Create the Scene**: Now that you are relaxed and much of the task driven mental clutter has been paused, think of the circumstances that you would like to practice. Let's use the example of the job interview. Now, to make it real I want you to ponder and practice every aspect of the interview, from the way you are dressed (you look stunning, by the way), to the feel of the firm handshake you receive when you meet your interviewer(s). Sit in the chair that they point to and politely accept, or decline, the offer of a glass of water. Now, as the interview begins, feel the confidence welling up inside as you expertly respond to each question they ask. See the interviewer(s) smiling and nodding as they take notes on your answers. Finally, sense everyone in the room, including yourself, feeling lighthearted and excited as the interview begins to wrap up. They love you! (And why wouldn't they! You are the perfect candidate for the role!)

3. **It's in the Details**: Create the same level of immersion for every aspect of your visualizations. See yourself

lifting heavier weights or running further with ease. Picture walking in your new kitchen and looking out the window with a hot cup of tea in your hand. Feel the hugs and high fives as your teammates respond to your ability to knock all ten pins down. The more detail you can contribute, the more real it will feel.

4. **Add Light**: It is important that you leave every visualization a success, as a happy realization of that which you seek. The best way to do that is to add light to your mental images at the end of your session. Using the example of a great job interview: Before you leave the room, surround the entire scene with light and love. Send the interviewer(s), the room, the chair, the windows, and yourself positive energy, love, light, and gratitude. This process of wrapping a scene in light and love enhances the experience and locks it into your brain in a way that takes it beyond simple visualization. The chemical response to love is significantly different than the chemical signature of a task completed, and I believe this addition will absolutely take your process to the next level!

5. **Celebrate**! After each visualization session, take a few moments to experience the celebratory feeling of a successful event! Feel a surge of excitement flow through your body as you realize that you are now

stepping into your dreams. You did it! Wow! Well done! Congratulations!

6. **Repeat Often:** The more you practice a desired skill, the more refined the skill becomes. Visualization is no different. Come back often, and each time add new layers of clarity to the experience. Use all your senses! How does it look, sound, smell, taste, feel? Who is in the scene? How does the room/location/pool/court/ring feel? What type of cologne or perfume are you wearing? Did I mention that you look fantastic? The more you can get into the visualization experience the more likely you will one day see, hear, and feel the goal in its manifested form. So, practice, practice, practice!

Additional Thoughts...

You may have noticed that I did not recommend that you be in a dark room for the process of visualization, though that is always helpful. You can effectively visualize at any moment, in any location. I know people that magnificently practice this skill while in a busy airport, rehearsing an important presentation, listening to soft music while waiting on a flight. I personally have successfully visualized everything from speeches to hitting the game winning home run in hectic, noise and people filled locations.

The point here is that it does not matter where you visualize, just that you do! What a life skill it is! This process can help you decrease anxiety, increase focus, and add joy and fulfillment to otherwise mundane experiences (like waiting at the airport). Give your smartphone and status updates a rest and go somewhere fun and productive in your mind. It will be well worth it!

Mindfulness, Signs, and Being Present

"And, when you want something, all the Universe conspires in helping you achieve it."

– Paulo Coehlo, "The Alchemist"

My hope is that by the time you get to this section of the book you have already had some decent meditation and visualization sessions. Or maybe you are already a master practitioner, which is fantastic! Either way, I cannot overstate the beauty and influence that these two exercises can have on your life. They slow down your thoughts, let your brain pause, help you clarify your goals, and open doors to ideas, people, encounters, and "signs" that you may have not previously seen.

Signs are very cool when you know what to look for! My son calls them synchronicities, things that happen when you are in tune with something that is important to you. I have had my fair share of synchronicities that have helped my journey, signs that were just too clear to ignore. When they happen, it is a fun way to validate a goal or a line of existing thought. As an example, one day Andrew and I were sitting in the back yard of our rented California house, enjoying a cold IPA and telling stories. I was sharing some of my thoughts regarding the future and the massive changes I was beginning to contemplate, like writing this book. I remember telling him, "*And I keep seeing crows along my path! Usually it's just one crow, which is unusual, because they typically travel in pairs. One crow means change, while two crows are a sign of good luck.*"

The moment I finished my statement, I heard a tell-take "caw," and we both looked up to watch a single crow fly right over us in a relaxed, diagonal path across our yard. We both immediately looked at each other and said, in perfect unison, "Whoa!" Andrew told me that he pretty much believed in the power of intention and synchronicity before that happened, but now he REALLY believed it! These are the types of events that are waiting for you once you clarify that which you are seeking.

Now that you have a goal, or maybe several, firmly locked in place, and you know that you can weave them into your **Focus**-centered life, it is time to explore the final step of this section. Come with me now as we explore the beauty of presence and mindfulness.

Presence and Mindfulness

You have heard these terms before: Being present, mindfulness, living in the now. There's a reason why these topics are on everyone's radar, and why even the uber successful, like Arianna Huffington and the Richard Gere, are practitioners and advocates. Even my favorite EDM DJ's Jahan and Yasmine Yousaf, aka "Krewella," talk about staying present and inner peace all the time. (And I love that about them!)

Being present is huge part of mindfulness. If you are constantly living in the memories of the past, or even day-dreaming about the compelling future you have imagined, you may forget to enjoy the beauty of the moments that surround you right now. After all, now is a product of your efforts in the past. Who you are, at this moment, is an aggregation of your previous thoughts, experiences, decisions, interactions, and beliefs about yourself. They have all led to this point in your existence! It took a lot of work to get here, so it's okay to slow down and enjoy where and who you are in this moment.

You might be thinking, "*Hold on a second there, Michelle. Haven't you been on your soap box about creating a compelling vision of the future? And didn't I just read an entire chapter dedicated to disconnecting so that you could visualize your goals? How does staying right where I am fit into those theories?*" It's a great question, and I can't blame you if you asked it! It has a lot to do with balance and doing the right thing at the right time. Allow me to illustrate this concept.

If you are in the middle of an important budget meeting at work, and your area is about to be highlighted in front of the leadership team, that is probably not the best time to visualize how it will feel to finally achieve your dream of a low score in golf. When in a conversation with others, whether it is a single person or a group, it's always a good idea to stay present. The same holds true for performing any complex task or effort. My hope was that the dentist who was working on my teeth that day was focused on his task while I was off in la-la land!

If you are in the shower, however, enjoying the warmth of the water, or winding down at the end of a productive day, sitting on your deck and enjoying the waning sunshine, it's totally the right time to enjoy the present moment while also letting your mind drift into those compelling ideas you have for the future. See? Right thing, right time.

You will find that with even the most compelling goals you will still spend most of your day focused on the present, in the moments of right now. The good news, kind of a bonus, is that when you are fully present you tend to notice more signs and synchronicities.

What is "Mindfulness"?

I once saw a graphic that illustrated how the word "mindfulness" has increased in utilization over the years. It was not a slow, gradual progression at all. Picture a hockey stick! Mindfulness was a flat line of minimal use from about 1800 through 1950. Then, according to the graph, the word began to take off, hitting a tipping point around 2008 when use of the word began to skyrocket! Whether it was because the financial crisis in the US that forced people into a deeper exploration of what was important, or it was just a topic that had earned it's time in the sun, I am thrilled that as a population many are in the "woke" status experienced today.

Mindfulness is defined as "*the quality or state of being conscious or aware of something.*" It is also described as, "*a mental state achieved by focusing one's awareness on the present moment, while calmly acknowledging and accepting one's feelings, thoughts, and bodily sensations.*" Perfect. We need more of this, right?

The benefits of being present, or mindful, are diverse, plentiful, and crazy cool. Individuals that are mindful, at least in my experience, seem to be happier in general. They generate more of a peaceful vibe and less of that frantic energy you sometimes feel with super busy and distracted people. In addition to vibing better energy, those who are mindful are more relatable friends, mentors, partners, coaches, and leaders. Doesn't it feel good when someone is present when they are with you? It's always a better experience than when someone is manically checking their cell phone, while insisting they are listening.

I committed years ago to working on being more present in conversations with others, whether they were friends, family members, co-workers, or even children. I do my level best to not be distracted by the phone dinging, or an email popping up. (I turned off notifications a long time ago. Those persistent buggers can wait their turn.) My goal is to be fully present and immersed in the conversation with whomever is in front of me. When I do, I know they get more out of the experience, and guess what? So do I! I even practice presence and mindfulness when I am playing with Nova. She can feel when I am distracted with other things, whether it is my phone, Netflix, or this beautiful iMac that sits in front of me as I write. She patiently waits her turn, but when it is "Nova time" I am all in, and she knows it.

Another benefit of mindfulness and staying present is that it keeps you from stewing about things that have happened in your past. We all have the tendency to look at previous events and recall how they made us feel, which usually falls into three general categories: nostalgic, depressed/angry/hurt, or deeply grateful. Our history is important, and it's fun to watch a fun memory sneak its way into the present. It's still better to focus on today, though, as it is also a whole lot easier to drive towards our goals and enjoy the road trip along the way when we are not staring into the rearview mirror.

"Mindfulness is a quality that's always been there. It's an illusion that there's a meditation and post-meditation period, which I always find amusing. Because you're either mindful or you're not."

– Richard Gere

In my enhanced state of a **Focus**, **Fulfilled** lifestyle, I am mindful of all my efforts and do all that I can to stay present, unless of course, I am intentionally working on visualization or meditation. So far, it has produced many results. Mindfulness and presence work for:

- The meeting
- The one on one conversation
- The phone conversation with mom
- Conversations with Andrew
- Walks with Nova
- My homework
- The get together or BBQ with friends
- The workout
- The chiropractor appointment
- Answering email
- Cooking (and eating) dinner
- Writing this book
- And so much more!

7-Day Mindfulness Challenge

If you believe, in theory, that being more present could help you live a more focused and fulfilled life, then allow me to introduce to you a 7-day challenge. Starting today, except for your meditation or visualization exercises, commit to being fully present in all your activities for the following week. Every single action, including: conversations with friends, family, co-workers and strangers, all your work meetings, making a meal, eating a meal, grocery shopping, working out, and taking time to read more of "Focused, Fit, and Fulfilled After 50!" Every time you feel your mind beg you to drift into thoughts of the past, or visions of the future, take a breath, and internally say the word "here." Unless you are in the dentist chair like I was earlier, "here" is usually a cool place if you give it your full attention.

As you navigate through the seven days, journal any thoughts that come up. How did being fully present feel? Was it difficult? Did you notice any difference in your ability to add value to a conversation or meeting? Did you get more out of it? Did you find yourself enjoying interactions more, or was your restless brain trying to pull you back to habitual thoughts of yesterday or tomorrow? What you once thought was boring or tedious may surprise you when you pay close attention. This may take some work, but I think you will agree that the effort is well worth it. It is your right to fully experience the fruits of your labor, and today is an integral part of your creation! Enjoy!

Now that we are in a good mental space and have found new ways to center and be present, while also feeling the compelling and soul provoking allure of a vision of the future, it is time to fuel the energy needed to manifest each one of your visual creations. The path to this ability is through the realm of fitness.

Section 2: The Five Elements of Fitness

I hope that by this point in the book you are starting to feel more centered, peaceful, and focused. Even incremental improvements have a way of compounding over time and catapulting you to heights you may not have previously attained. Assuming you are now fully focused and ready for more, it is time to shift from an inward-focused mindset to the way our physical body feels and how it can help us reach all the goals we have placed in front of us.

Much like my approach to improving focus, I knew I needed to find new ways to push the fifty-year-old physical manifestation of "Michelle" to new dimensions of strength. The same old routine would give me the same old results. It wasn't going to work if I simply tried harder, worked out more, or drank fewer IPA's. I needed a holistic approach to health that looked at all aspects of my life, and I believe I have found it. I would like to introduce you to what I call "The Five Elements of Fitness."

The Five Elements of Fitness

Months before I started this process, I thought, *I'm in decent shape for my age.* I took pride in the fact that when I shared how old I was with someone the typical reaction was "*No way. Really? I never would have guessed that!*" Whether or not they were just being kind, or didn't know what a fifty-year-old should look like, is irrelevant. I let is stroke my ego and satiate me with a temporary hit of satisfaction. Then, inevitably, I would have a day where looking in the mirror would cause a *what the hell!* reaction. I saw the smudged, dark shadows under my tired looking eyes, lines creeping into my mouth and chin, and a slight rounding forward of my shoulders, as if standing up straight just wasn't worth the effort anymore. I am still not sure what over-fifty is supposed to feel like, but those cringe-worthy mirror moments were not something I wanted to continue. Nope, uh-uh, no way.

My active, focused brain, and excited, driven soul had more to accomplish, and I was convinced that the difference was energy! Consistent, natural, peak energy! Not the caffeine-induced buzz that barely got me though some days. I had to find a better way to approach the physical part of my life.

The breaking point came during a stretch when I was traveling a ton for business, feeling I had no time for anything outside of the rhythm of work, eat, sleep, repeat. Occasionally, I would throw in a token stretch or do a few sit-ups in my hotel room, but nothing of substance. I had things to do, right? Oh, I still had the goals and the big dreams, but I didn't have the energy to tackle them. *"Not right now,"* I told myself, somewhat convincingly. *"Soon. Right now, just keep your head above water!"* I didn't even have the motivation to play and recharge on the weekend. You know it's bad when you can't even muster the energy to relax! Seriously! I was beginning to feel the slow, insidious slide into aging, watching my energy, focus, and sense of wonder decline incrementally year after year after year. Was this really it? Were all my aspirations and goals behind me? Was the future simply more work sprinkled with occasional moments of joy attached to vacations, a new puppy, a grandchild someday, a promotion at work, or a new car/computer/purchase? Was the rest of my time simply getting from one day to another without too much angst or stress, living in the center of my self-imposed "comfort zone?" The realization that I was truly slipping into that future scared the shit out of me and was part of the catalyst for change.

Once I made the concrete decision to transform, the **Five Elements of Fitness** came to me fluidly. Through trial and error, I have refined each element, seeing what worked and what didn't. If something gave me more energy, it stayed in my routine. If I tried it and my energy crashed, out the door it went. Simple.

Ultimately, I discovered that I needed all five elements, working together, to experience the massive increase in energy that I feel today. The interrelated, symbiotic **Five Elements of Fitness** are:

1. Sound Sleep
2. My Relationship with Food
3. Water Works
4. Movement (Just Move)!
5. Stretching for Connection and Decompression

Notice that I didn't just list "Food" as the second element. While gastronomy choices do matter, and I will offer my recommendations on what may propel you towards your goals, I believe shifting my relationship with food was even more important than the actual food I choose to ingest!

Each of these elements is critically important to overall health, and respectively carry with them a chance to create significant change in the quality of life. The game changer, for me, was incorporating them all into a *lifestyle* that became an integral part of who I am today. The new me! I sincerely believe that the key is this: *How I sleep, eat, hydrate, and move is a lifestyle. When these habits changed in a cohesive way, the standard of my health shifted dramatically!*

I hope you will come on this journey with me and weave all five elements through your life. If you pick and choose, and only do one or two, such as work your ass off at the gym and stretch every day, but rarely sleep well and compensate for this deficiency with caffeine and energy drinks, it's less likely you will see the full results of this adjustment. It's also more difficult if we continue to stress and fatigue our adrenals via a lifestyle with a near frantic daily pace. If that's where you are, however, much respect to you, as I have been there myself, and sometimes the demands of this world can feel time and energy consuming. Maybe you could consider easing one element in at a time, and if it works for you, and frees up a little more energy, try another. There's no right or wrong approach here. Find what works for you!

I believe that sleep, water, food, and movement are as interdependent as the players on a high-performing basketball team. Or as a horse and rider in a barrel race. When they are working together, and things are really clicking, it is a beautiful thing to behold. With that in mind, let's dive into the first of the five elements!

Sound Sleep

"Sleep is the best meditation."

– Dalai Lama

You may be raising one eyebrow right now, speculating, *"Why, Michelle, are you starting the section on movement with a chapter on remaining still? If sleep is the first thing that comes to* *mind when you think of '**Fitness**,' then maybe the years really are catching up to you!*"

I am beginning this section with a missive on healthy sleep because I believe that a solid, uninterrupted, unaided (medically speaking) night of slumber is the ultimate daily reboot for a Focused, Fit, and Fulfilled life. A chance to reset, refresh, and recharge mentally, physically, and emotionally. We all need sleep, because if we are not resting at night, we are pressing our body deeper into patterns of fight or flight, stress-fueled days that require tons of compensatory behaviors. (Think caffeine, sugar highs, and other stimulants that simply mask what is really needed.) It's also a quick way to fast track some of the major health related lifestyle diseases. No one wants that.

I sleep like a champ most nights, and rarely struggle to nod off. I'm still not one of those accomplished individuals who can sleep soundly on a flight or in the car, but in a bed, with a squishy, cool, feather pillow under my head, yup, I'm good to go. I haven't always slept well though. For years falling asleep was a chore I dreaded, a game I tried, and often failed, to win. That sought-after deep REM sleep was not going to happen unless I fooled my mind into believing it was ready to rest. Sometimes, I resorted to having a little something to help me knock out. I never "graduated" to prescription sleep aids, but I had my dances with melatonin (the natural remedy?) and other over the counter, not intended for frequent use solutions. One of them had acetaminophen in it, and I have to tell you, the thought of taking a NSAID now, just because it was glued to the formula for helping me fall asleep, makes me close my eyes and shake my head.

Inevitably, I would get the sleep aid "fog" the next morning, creating a desire for more caffeine. Lots of it. It's no wonder I struggled to nod off with that buzz racing through my veins. Power up! Power down. Power up! Power down. No judgement, younger version of me, it was part of your journey and you know better now. You can also sleep without it.

Why Can Sleep Be So Elusive?

For some, there can be medical reasons for insomnia, and the amount of caffeine ingested during the day may have an impact as well. In my life, however, the factors were pretty cut and dry and were usually caused by me and me alone. When I was not sleeping well on a consistent basis, the recommended seven-nine hours every night, the three contributing influences that held me back from a restful somnolence were:

1. My habits in the evening
2. Stress
3. The thoughts I chose to focus on

A majority of my sleeping difficulties resided in the third point. I had the tendency to stew on the wrong thoughts a lot. It wasn't that I didn't believe I could sleep. It had everything to do with having a mind that wouldn't rest or stay present. If I wasn't going over mental checklists of things I needed to do, I was fretting about work, or how I was going to "get it all done" as a single mother with a full-time job. I spent loads of time spinning about the past and worrying about the future. I could hold onto a single destructive thought and chew on it for hours, allowing it to float through my thoughts in an endless loop, like a scratched record that keeps playing the part of the song you don't even like. In my estimation, this state of having a swirling mind is probably responsible for ninety-percent of my sleeplessness.

Once, I spent an entire night getting myself completely worked up over two sentences in a single conversation earlier in the day. A complete night! I replayed the dialogue in my head over and over again, drawing one dramatic conclusion after another. I was nearly sick to my stomach from all the adrenaline pumping into it as I tried desperately to shut my mind off. Nothing worked, not exercise, not a beer, not even watching TV or reading. Halfway through the night, or should I say early morning, I exercised again, took a shower, and drank another beer, hoping it would lull me to sleep. It didn't. Daylight finally came, and a little after seven am, I made a call to the person I was fretting about, hoping to get some clarity on the dialogue that had eviscerated my night. In approximately two minutes, the air was clear, and I realized I had taken those two measly statements completely out of context. I felt relieved, exhausted, and foolish. *Has this ever happened to you? Have you ever lost sleep over swirling thoughts?*

Michelle Baker

Pivoting to Good Sleep

What changed? How did I break the vicious circle of sleep aids and foggy mornings, followed by caffeine, caffeine, and more caffeine? How did I get my active mind to slow down and take a much-needed break? Ultimately, I decided that not sleeping well at night, and burning out my adrenals during the day, was simply not sustainable. It was wrecking my peace, my body, and nerves. I needed a shift, and I was desperate to find a medication-free solution.

Initially, I tried watching movies I had seen many times before, hoping the familiarity would lull me into slumber. My brother Tom called this practice "Apollo PM," since Apollo 13 was one of those go-to favorites. That worked occasionally, but I am convinced I rarely reached a subterranean REM-like state with the TV on. I moved on to meditative recordings designed to help quiet the mind, but the earphones always became uncomfortable and kept me from getting beyond a surface level snooze.

At my wits end, (probably due to the lack of sleep), I chose to throw it all out the window and create a method that would work consistently, no matter where I happened to call it a night. After a ton of practice, with some hits and misses, the steps listed below are what work for me. To this day, I use this practice to achieve a peaceful night of rest and recovery. It's simple and straight-forward, yet it has proven ninety-five percent effective for me. Here's what I do every night, whether I am at home or traveling:

1. **Bed "Time" Consistency**. Having a consistent time to go to sleep works wonders. It aligns my body and brain in an expected routine that becomes wired into my circuitry. My circadian rhythm, also known as the body's "internal clock", is set in such a way that it knows when it's time to reduce brain activity and begin the process of overnight mental and physical recovery. It also knows when it's beneficial to wake up and begin the day, which is why I can get up without an alarm. Unless I'm jumping time zones I am almost always in bed around nine pm. Bedtime for you may be much later, and that's okay as long as it's consistent. In my world, unless there is something unusual going on, my routine is to begin slowing down and getting ready for bed around eight pm, with a goal of lights out an hour later. A contributing factor to this early time frame is that I am a bona fide morning person. Yep, one of those! Early to bed, early to rise makes me happy. Having this routine trains my brain that a few hours after dinner it needs to begin the slide into recuperation mode. If every night was a different story, and my mind didn't know what to expect, it would be a lot harder to convince my brain that it was time to sleep.

2. **Winding Down**: A flowing, relaxing, decompressing, and *consistent* nighttime routine makes a huge difference. Human beings do not have an on/off switch.

We typically do not go from racing around in a mode of task completion to fast asleep and resting within moments, although, I have seen babies and toddlers pull off this remarkable feat. Adults need time to transition from pushing our minds and bodies in a peak state, to recognition that it is time to clock out and slow down. The best way to do this, in my experience, is to make the last hour of my waking day a peaceful one, with limited mental or physical stressors. I mentioned earlier that I like to do a power hour of productivity at night, but this usually happens right after dinner. I limit physical exertion, and I avoid anything that may create a negative emotional connection, such as reading the news or scrolling through too much social media (which often reflects what is in the news). Screen time in general *activates* my mind, and I am trying to do just the opposite. Instead, I start to put things away from the day and take Nova outside where we can both take a breath and stretch. I may chat with Andrew about the next day, change into my PJ's, and vibe gratitude for my life. Bottom line, I make the last waking hour as stress free and *non-mentally stimulating* as possible.

3. **Story Time**: When I was a child, like most kids, I loved to have stories read to me. I eagerly floated into the world of fantasy and make believe, heroes and villains, and of course, happy endings. I continue that practice

today by reading stories, in the form of fantastic novels, at night to help me sleep. In my waking hours, my reading consumption is always books centered around enrichment, business, and philosophy. My two favorite works of all time are *Atlas Shrugged* by Ayn Rand, and *The Alchemist,* by Paulo Coehlo. If you haven't read them yet, I encourage you to do so, though Atlas is a summer-long commitment for most. The Alchemist can be read in a weekend, though don't mistake the brevity for a lack of depth. It's a classic. When I read at night, as good as these books are, my goal is not to get into deep contemplation but to escape thoughts in general. I want to immerse myself in someone else's tale of love, struggle, victory, and perseverance. My favorite books right now are the *Outlander* series by Diana Gabaldon. I have also read the *Twilight* franchise, and a bit of *Harry Potter*. It only takes twenty minutes of reading most nights and I can feel my brain slipping into a beautiful light sleep. I wait until I am starting to nod off, turn the light out, and let my thoughts just drift. I don't try to direct my contemplations at this point, I just let go. Unless something interrupts this slide, I am out, and deep sleep is not far behind.

4. **White Noise**: When I worked on ships, initially it was hard to sleep with any consistency. We were usually

sailing at night, steaming from one port to the next for the touring pleasure of our passengers. This meant near constant movement and noise. While I was onboard, I discovered the benefit of ear plugs and the sound of a fan. Currently, I am in a quieter environment yet still use both resources when I sleep. The consistency and repetitive nature of white noise makes it easy for my brain to block it out, simultaneously hindering any sounds that might be occurring nearby, and ear plugs reduce noise even more. I do not recommend ear plugs and white noise for anyone that needs to listen for, say, a sleeping infant, but for me this combination has proven to be a winner.

Mitigating Interruptions: Nova snores. She sleeps in her dog bed in the corner of my room, and some nights, if her head is at just the right angle, she can get a pretty robust rumble going. The sound and vibration have often yanked me out of that gradual slide between light and deep sleep, bringing me right back to the surface where I started. Have you ever had that experience? Drifting, drifting, drifting, about to tip into that blissful realm of sleep, and something happens to snap you out of it? It sucks! My old response to this used to be absolute frustration, especially when I was not sleeping well. "*I was so close!*" I would think. "*This is not fair!*" Well, those thoughts aren't going to land the plane. I would get myself so worked up that's it's no wonder I struggled to fall asleep again.

5. Now when Nova snores at the wrong time, or I hear a noise that gets my attention, I take a different approach. It's still not fun for this slide to be interrupted, but I realize I can get to sleep much quicker if I recognize it, acknowledge the disruption, and *here's the key*, I send it love. Yes, love! No matter what the distraction was, I have discovered that when I pivot to love and appreciation, and not allow my mind to get sucked into emotions that cause adrenaline like frustration, anger, and sadness, I can easily obtain a restful state again. Usually, I don't even remember drifting off because it happens so quickly. And if it doesn't, and Nova snores one more time, I just remember how glad I am that she's there, safe in her bed, present in my life. Occasionally, I also get up and physically adjust her head for her too.

I now look forward to sleeping at night. I get so much out of this restful time and know that it fuels my ability to achieve the goals I have set for myself, including peak levels of fitness. I urge you, with love and empathy for your sleep struggles if you have them, to find a routine that works for your mind, and for that irreplaceable body.

"There's practically no element of our lives that's not improved by getting adequate sleep."

– Arianna Huffington

Relationship with Food

For some readers, this is the chapter you have been waiting for. Maybe you even jumped ahead and came right here! If you did, I completely get it, as I have impatiently done the same technique before. Have you ever gotten sucked into one of those online ads that promised "eat these three foods and it will change your life?" Or, "these five foods cause massive inflammation?" Thirty minutes into the video you know what vitamin the doctor is selling but are still wondering what the heck the foods are! *"Just tell me what to eat already! What's the magic formula?!"*

If you did fast forward to this chapter, I promise you this: no gimmicks, no broken promises, and hopefully no frustration-based lack of sharing. Just a straight-forward approach to this inclusive (everybody eats), emotionally charged (we will get to that) topic of what to put in your now focused, driven body. I also cover what I HIGHLY recommend avoiding as frequently as possible. I do this by way of sharing *paradigm shifts* that helped me lose unwanted fat, significantly increased my energy, and dramatically reduced the impact of spikes, dips, and cravings related to changes in blood sugar.

Before we get deeper into the concepts that helped me change, I need to share with you one of my truths. I HAD to get over the *guilt* that I sometimes associated with eating before anything else would work. I don't know why I ever had this response to a meal, or why even a healthy outing would occasionally cause me to feel sluggish and reach for more caffeine. I just often related the normal state of slowing down to begin the digestive process with a sense that I had messed up. This guilt was impacting my ability to both enjoy my meals and process them in the best way.

To clarify, this did not happen with every meal, or even every day. I have enjoyed an average weight for a long time now, and many have even described me as thin. The sense of overindulging did happen though, and I knew I needed to fix that first. Once I removed the guilt, regardless of what I chose to eat, my health results accelerated. It's that simple.

If you don't believe me try this. For the next three days eat as you normally would. Same meals, same portions, same timing. Change only one thing: As you are eating each meal, internally express appreciation. Appreciation for the ability to afford that food, appreciation for the taste, even appreciation for how quickly the fast food team member processed your order! When the slow down comes after the meal, appreciate that too, picturing your body turning what you ate into energy. After three days of no other change, save that one, see how you feel.

Paradigm Shifts on Eating – The Beliefs I HAD to Change!

As we dive into the belief systems that I modified, in a big way, to create massive improvements in my health, I want to share one quick note. I cannot state with more resolve that every <u>body</u> is different. I highly encourage you to test the concepts that make sense and adjust according to the results that you experience. What is outlined in the next few chapters is not the only right way. There are many. My hope is that by sharing my journey, my experiences, my wins and losses, it will inspire you to begin your own process of exploration. With that said, on to the paradigm shifts!

Paradigm #1

From: "The right diet or detox will finally fix me."
To: "Healthy eating is a *lifestyle*! I'm playing the long game!"

The idea of a "long game" is a concept that has led me to more viable change than all of the other shifts combined. It is also the one that helped me achieve sustainable, lasting results, and an awakening about the real role of food in my life. This concept required a significant mindset transformation, a commitment to change, and the willingness to permanently let go of beliefs that wouldn't, and never did, serve me. I said goodbye to the principle that with the right amount of discipline, denial, and calorie counting I could finally, this time for sure, beat the odds and watch the weight magically disappear. It never really did in any

82

significant way. Ultimately, I decided that: *I will never "diet" again. Instead, I am making holistic lifestyle changes!*

I'm in this for the long haul! The changes I have already made to my daily routine, relationship with food, and nutritional choices helped me pivot my health and energy from "just OK" to "pretty damn good." It all started with the realization that quick fix diets, fasts, and cleanses are not the solution for long term results. While occasional reboots (cleanses and detoxes) are great from time to time, they work best for me when my body is already in a healthy state.

I know all about fasts, because I have tried quite a few. Juice fasts, keto fasts, seven-day detoxes, and even the well-known cayenne pepper master cleanse. They all produced temporary results, and I shed excess water weight and felt good after a few days, but within weeks I was right back to where I started. And then some. The challenge was that each of them worked in the short term, but none of them solved the underlying issues that had created the extra weight in the first place.

When I decided to pursue peak levels of health after I began fleshing out the concepts of a Focus, Fit, and Fulfilled lifestyle, I experimented with a few new approaches to eating. Keto and paleo were on the list, because I knew protein gave me longer term energy than the spikes associated with a more carb-filled approach. I even tried a vegetarian lifestyle, which I totally respect and admire, but I never mastered the blood sugar balance without the animal-based protein. I eventually landed on a balanced regimen that focused not on the quick fix, but on a daily practice of eating to provide energy.

What was this perfect combination of food choices? The right balance of protein, carbs, and fats? Everyone is going to have a different perfect answer to this question. While salmon and sushi may work wonders for one person, another might thrive on chicken and broccoli, while still another may see massive improvements going completely vegan. I am going to share in the chapters ahead what worked for me, and I encourage you to experiment with what works for you. I will share foods I had to eliminate for good, and choices that consistently give me clean, sustainable energy. The purpose of this paradigm shift is to know that changing your holistic approach to eating, and not looking for a quick win, is always going to provide better results. I'm committed to the long game, choosing to do my best every day to make choices that made me feel good. Period.

Paradigm #2

From: "Counting calories and fat grams is my primary focus."
To: "My relationship with food is my primary focus!"

My Relationship with Food

I have had an on-again, off-again, *positive* relationship with eating. We are in a solid, happy place now (thank you for asking), but it wasn't always this way. Recently, I came to the realization that if I did not fix my rapport with food *first,* then even the best combination of food choices would not serve me. *I believe that how you eat, and how you feel WHEN you eat, is as important or more so than WHAT you choose to ingest.*

How is that possible? Don't calories, fat grams, carbs, and proteins really determine how much weight we lose? Not as much as you would think. Believe it or not, and hopefully through this material you are beginning to believe, your mental state and beliefs towards eating have a tremendous impact on your food assimilation process. That, in turn, can have a dramatic impact on your ability to reach your fitness goals. Allow me to explain.

You've Got Nerve!

I promise not to get too geeky on this topic, but it's important to cover the basics as I understand them. In a nutshell, our digestion is impacted, positively or negatively, by how we trigger our autonomic nervous system (ANS). The ANS is a control system for many of our unconscious bodily functions, such as heart rate, respiration, and, you guessed it, digestion. There are three different aspects of the ANS, all of which have the capacity to effect how we assimilate food:

1. **Parasympathetic Nervous System (PNS)**: Controls bodily processes such as digestion, cellular repair, and overall relaxation.

2. **Sympathetic Nervous System (SNS)**: Most commonly known for its ability to trigger the "fight or flight" response. This system redirects blood flow away from digestion to the brain and muscles so that we can respond to an emergency situation, real or imagined. Stress is a common trigger for the SNS.

3. **Enteric Nervous System (ENS):** Sometimes referred to as the "second brain," it governs the overall function of our gastrointestinal tract.

You may be wondering how a working knowledge of your ANS can help you achieve your health and fitness goals. I was too! When I leaned into this valuable lesson, it was one of the many game changers I discovered as I progressed along this journey.

Here are the basics:

When we are relaxed before, during, and after a meal, we enable our parasympathetic and enteric nervous systems to *operate at maximum efficiency.* When they operate at maximum efficiency, we digest easily, assimilating our food into a form that can be utilized for energy. If we eat in a state of stress (remember, stress triggers fight or flight), or fall into a mode of guilt or anger (at ourselves) after the meal, our brain activates the sympathetic nervous system. When this happens, it directs *blood AWAY from the digestive process* and towards those areas where the mind perceives we may need it to fight, or to run. Amazing! So, if we are stressed before, during, or after a meal, we are not assimilating or digesting our food with any degree of effectiveness. This alone can add unwanted pounds to our body!

You might be thinking that you are not typically "stressed" while you eat. In fact, you feel darn good after a meal. If that's the case, perfect! Keep it up! For most meals, even before my shift, I felt this way too. But if you ever feel guilt for eating the "wrong" foods, just know that this guilt could be exacerbating the impact of an already heavy meal. In a nutshell, if you choose the double cheeseburger at the new local gastropub (grass-fed beef I hope!), just enjoy the treat! It's better for your body, and your mood!

This one adjustment, eliminating negative feelings attached to eating, can have a dramatic effect on your health, and your weight. I wish I had known that one years ago! It would have saved me a ton of angst, and probably a few pounds as well. Here were some of my past "relationship with food" misdeeds.

Have you ever:

- Felt guilty immediately after a meal, even when it was mostly healthy?
- Avoided a treat that looked appealing then caved later in the day and ate two, feeling a sense of deprivation?
- Sensed the normal energy dip after a meal and reached for additional caffeine?
- Made one food choice misstep, admonished yourself, and decided to "start fresh tomorrow," eating three times as much as you needed the rest of the day?

- Made food choices based on that vicious circle of blood sugar highs and lows?

My supposition is that we need to fix this internal relationship with food before we can both enjoy the process of eating and have food serve us in the way it was meant to. My hope is that the following pages will set you on a course to do just that.

Why is Food so Emotional?

Our relationship with food probably started at an early age, and the positive and negative behaviors that serve us, or don't, are reinforced by our thoughts and choices every day. Food is used to nourish us, to celebrate big events, and to console us after disappointments or loss. Most social gatherings are centered around food. We date around meals, and we build memories around creating edible memories, like making sugar cookies with Grandma at Christmas time. It isn't the sweet indulgence of eating the cookie afterwards that makes those celebrations lasting and cherished, it's the memory created during the process, the moments now instantly captured for Facebook and Instagram.

People love to talk about food! If you want to stop productivity in the workplace, or get a healthy debate started when out with friends, talk about food. Most individuals have a wide and varied set of opinions related to gastronomy, like what tastes best, which foods are best for you, as well as the "must try" recipes that will make you the star of the next gathering.

The bottom line on this paradigm is to enjoy each meal, and those you choose to share them with, knowing that no one meal, or day of deprivation, is going to make or break your results. Revel in that fact that we are surrounded by healthy, tasty, fulfilling options, and feel gratitude for the role that food plays in your life. My hope is that the rest of the paradigms will help in this regard.

Paradigm #3

From: "I'm too busy to slow down and eat."

To: "I'll always have time to slow down and eat!"

Have you ever wondered why it feels like a badge of honor to say, "*I'm just so busy?*" It's as if that statement loosely translates into "*I am so important,*" or something to that effect. I used to believe that I was too busy, on most days, to stop what I was doing and enjoy my lunch at work. I would eat at my desk, door closed, reading email, or quickly checking the news headlines. Half the time I ate so fast I could barely remember how it tasted, and I rarely gave my stomach enough time to trigger the "satisfied" button. Being too busy to slow down and enjoy my meal is now, for me, comparable to saying, "*I am too busy to be healthy.*" That is no longer true in my life, which is why this paradigm has forever shifted.

Most of us will always have time to slow down and eat, because it doesn't take that long to enjoy most meals. While a twenty to thirty-minute mealtime is ideal, even focusing on how good a ten-minute repast feels will create lasting change. And who doesn't have ten minutes? This approach is profoundly impactful, yet it is potentially one of the easiest to enact. Here are some simple meal timing hacks to get you moving in the right direction:

- **Focus on Your Meal**. I get it, we live in a world full of mental stimulation. It is common to eat a meal in front of a screen of some sort, small or large, shared or individual. When I eat this way, I am more prone to trigger the SNS (think stress response) because of something I read in an email, saw on social, or read in the news. When I pause long enough to really enjoy my meal, I am more likely to stay relaxed, increase the efficacy of digestion, while also savoring my food.

- **Chewing:** Digestion starts in the mouth, and how you chew food has a dramatic impact on digestion. It can also impact your enjoyment level! Chew each bite at least twenty times, relishing the flavor that often gets deeper the longer you chomp. Why would you not want to experience that? As parents around the world always told us "Chew your food!"

- **Slow your roll**: Meals eaten on the run are sure to trigger or sustain the fight or flight stress response. Slow down. Unless you are running a half-marathon and downing one of those surgery power gels, make sure you take time to eat each meal. How can you stretch out a meal? Put your utensil down between bites. Take a deep breath. Try to feel how full you are. Focus on the appreciation for that meal. Take a sip of water. It takes seven to ten minutes for your brain to recognize that you are satiated. If you are eating unconsciously, or rapidly shoveling food in, your brain doesn't have time to recognize the signals of fullness. So, slow your roll!

- **The 80/20 rule**: Because it takes seven to ten minutes for your brain to process that you are full, a wonderful guideline I use is to only eat until I am about eighty percent full. By the time my brain catches up, that number will be closer to ninety or ninety-five percent. How do you know you are eighty percent full? You feel satisfied, but not stuffed. You can feel the impact of your stomach stretching out, but it's not uncomfortable. If you are at that point stop. Just stop. I can't tell you how many times I have made an amazing meal and felt disappointment that halfway through I was already at eighty percent. That's normal. I remind myself that I am playing the long game, and leftovers for lunch are a lovely idea.

5 Quick Tips to Make Every Meal More Aligned!

1. **Pause** before the first bite and vibe **appreciation** for what you are about to eat. Even a cheeseburger could use a little love.
2. **Chew** every bite at least twenty times. Not only does it **intensify** the flavor, it aids in digestion by breaking down the food even more.

3. **Take a break** every three or four bites. Put the fork down, drop the fries, let the veggie burrito rest. This allows your body to *catch up* and let you know how full you really are.

4. **Remember to breathe**. Not only does this help reduce stress when you are eating, oxygen is important in the digestive process.

5. **Stay present.** Eating a nice meal is a lovely experience, whether you are with others or chilling by yourself. Stay present with your food and *leave the screens alone* for the duration.

Paradigm #4

From: "Tomorrow is a fresh start to my diet."

To: "Every day, and every meal, is a chance to nourish my body and my soul!"

Before I started my Focus, Fit, and Fulfilled journey in earnest, I maintained a decent, but not ideal, weight. I was probably ten pounds over where I wanted to be, though I hid it well behind my Ann Taylor business suits during the day, and oversized sweatpants and t-shirts at night. I was skinny when I worked on ships, and rail thin when I was doing chores several times a day on the farm, but for most of my years the ten extra pounds were a part of my life. In my fifties it threatened to get worse. I was getting a little squishy in the middle, and arthritis was building up in my hands, shoulders, and knees. Not ideal for the energetic state I was seeking. In reflection, many of those pounds can be traced to one negative behavior, which I call the Tomorrow Syndrome. Does the following pattern sound familiar?

The Tomorrow Syndrome

I often found myself in a decent run of days where I had leveled out the blood sugar highs and lows, made healthy food choices, and overall felt good. An opportunity would then come along to indulge a bit, which, after all, I deserved, right? I would cave and accept the croissant, kettle chips, chicken wings, or the amazing tableside guacamole with a never-ending bowl of house made tortillas chips, washed down with an IPA. Yum! Any of these choices, in and of themselves, would not have significantly derailed my progress, or even added on some extra pounds. For me, however, I had this nasty habit of believing I would *start fresh tomorrow*. Instead of just eating the tableside guac and an IPA, I also ate too large a meal, had another IPA or two, then indulged in a sweet treat like one of those New Orleans inspired beignets with powdered sugar! Because, after all, tomorrow was going to be *perfect*! Tomorrow was going to change everything! Tomorrow I was finally going to get on the right path, this time for good!

I believe that a majority of the extra weight I have carried over the years has been as a result of this destructive pattern of "tomorrow I will start again."

Breaking the Syndrome

I came to grips with the fallacy that tomorrow was any different than today. The weight I carry is truly a culmination of ALL the choices I make over time. I no longer fall into the pit of overindulging after I make the conscious choice to treat myself. I'm done. When I decide to enjoy an experience by choosing a food item that I wouldn't necessarily eat every day, I fully immerse myself in the enjoyment of that item. I am thankful that most days are closer to normal, and I don't fall into this trap anymore. I am now kind to myself when I decide to have a little fun and just roll with it.

Paradigm #5

From: "Everything in moderation."

To: "Certain things in moderation. Everything else is binary (yes/no)!"

Shifting to a long-game, focus, fulfilled lifestyle still allows me to indulge from time to time. If I stressed about every single morsel that entered my body, counting calories, fat grams, carbs, trans fats, sugars, etc., it would be hard to reach my goals, not to mention be unenjoyable. I need to incorporate guilt-free moments into this wonderful life. For example, when visiting New York City, the walking alone should burn more calories than I can consume, but even without the exercise I know there are food choices that will be difficult to pass up. In my experience there is something special about having a slice of gooey pizza in the heart of Times Square!

I used to believe that I could have everything, no matter what it was, in moderation, if I didn't overindulge. I now believe that most foods, yes, including pizza, can be enjoyed in this way. There are some foods, however, that I try to avoid at all costs, because the impact on my body is just too severe. Here are the foods that work for me All the Time (Yes); In Moderation (Sometimes); and Never (No).

"All the Time" Choices

Some food groups and eating habits are obviously good for you. All the foods listed below are integrated into my regular routine and make me feel amazing. This list is not by any means comprehensive, but is representative of the shift that gave me a boatload of new energy.

- **Blueberries:** Growing up, I preferred fruits and vegetables to candy bars and donuts. Still do, though I have shifted my intake of fruit quite a bit. I find now that too much fruit tends to spike, and then crash, my blood sugar, especially on an empty stomach. The awesome superfood blueberries don't have that effect. I toss them on salads, in my yogurt, even in a smoothie or two. Of course, they play a starring role when, on occasion, I crave a bowl of oatmeal. I nearly always buy organic, which is harder to do in the off season, but no matter what they are in my shopping cart every week.

- **Broccoli**: Steamed or sautéed broccoli is a staple at my dinner table. Who doesn't love some al dente, bright green broccoli? Weighing in at just thirty calories and packing almost three grams of protein per serving, broccoli provides a nice balance to the lean protein and carb portions of the meal. Every feast should have a little green in it!

- **Green Salad**: I enjoy a fun, healthy salad almost every day! Kale, spinach, and arugula are my go-tos, though I also like to mix in a portion (about 1/3) of either iceberg lettuce or romaine for the added crunch and water value. I usually throw in some chopped red peppers, cucumbers, blueberries, or mandarin orange wedges too. I top it off with a few crumbles of goat cheese or feta, and a few almonds, walnuts, or pistachios. Salad for me is not only a yes, it's an everyday choice. I highly recommend being VERY careful about your choice of dressing, as well as the quantity, as this can take your salad from "super food" to "super bad."
  - o My dressing is usually a small amount of locally grown olive oil with balsamic vinegar. I always

steer clear of vegetable, peanut, and canola oils, as they are usually the culprit that kicks a salad into the super bad category!

- **Sweet Potatoes:** In a hurry while making dinner one night, I improvised a way to cook some sweet potatoes, and it was such a hit I now make it at least once a week. I melt some butter in a pan, sauté some onions, add a little sea salt, then add shaved sweet potatoes to the mix. (A wide potato peeler works wonders)! The thin slices cook in a matter of minutes and add a healthy carb option to our meal.

- **Amazing Grass Green Superfood Energy (Lemon Lime),** with juice from half a lemon. I don't recommend many name brands throughout this book, but this food is such a presence in my life I just have to! I discovered Amazing Grass when I worked on ships and needed epic amounts of energy that coffee alone could not provide. A peer introduced me to AG, (Thank you Dustin!) and I have had it every single day since 2013. It contains all the green superfoods (spirulina, wheat grass, and more) while also providing a caffeine kick from the green tea. It is my go-to way to start the day, with no acidic side effects I sometimes experienced with coffee. Andrew starts his day this way too and has experienced similar positive effects!

- **Eggs**: This compact dose of protein has been a great way to break my intermittent fast without slowing me down and causing any guilt-related issues. If I am at work, I bring along a hard-boiled egg or two, or sometimes I grab an egg-white omelet in the cafeteria. If I am dining out for breakfast, whether on a business trip or visiting with friends, omelets provide a filling protein option that I can dress up with all sorts of veggies, cheese, and yes, bacon! I stay away from the white flour, sugar-packed pancakes, French toast, Danishes, and buttered toast, as these all tend to slow me down. Though I don't eat eggs every day, they are on my personal "yes" list.

- **Lean Meat**: While I have tried completely shifting to vegan and vegetarian menus, and I believe they work wonders for some, my body craves a variety of salty, protein-based options to keep my blood sugar from spiking and crashing. This is where lean meats work well. For breakfast, I really love a little ham or bacon with my eggs for sustainable energy, and at night we almost always fill one third of the plate with a trim protein source. Unless I'm traveling this lean meat *has* to be from a local or organic source, such as Whole Foods, my go-to for all meat-related products! It is well worth the extra few dollars you will spend.

- **Greek Yogurt**: Love this option for breakfast once or twice a week now! I choose plain yogurt (sugar free) from grass-fed cows whenever possible. I add a handful of superfood blueberries or a drizzle of honey and I am good to go. It's a great protein source and super clean.

Extra "Yes" Tips

- **Dinner**: As mentioned above, a majority of my dinners include a lean, happy protein, and I always add a green side (salad or broccoli, the occasional asparagus), and either sweet potato hash or steamed rice. Chickpea pasta is also a nice alternative. I haven't made regular potatoes or semolina pasta since I began this new chapter, and I can really feel the difference. Starches, breads, and other heavy carbs take me straight to that lethargic, heavy feeling which I am trying to avoid. We drink unsweetened almond milk instead of soda, dairy milk, or soy, and our sweet side is usually a dash of applesauce. Simple. Clean.
- **Dessert**: Most nights a few dark chocolate nibs (darker the better) mixed with almonds, pistachios, or walnuts serve as a nice palate change. Sweet and savory!
- **Flax Seed Shot**: I discovered this through one of my health coach classes and I love the digestive difference it has made! I take a teaspoon of ground flax seed in a

shot glass full of water, stir it up, and drink it down twice a day, usually first thing in the morning then right before I go to bed. This one simple hack can positively change your elimination habits, and while that is not a topic anyone likes to talk about often, we all know it matters! The natural fiber keeps things moving and it helps keep blood sugar balanced until mid-morning.

- **Intermittent Fasting**: I have embraced the concept of intermittent fasting, refraining from eating, most days, from seven pm until nine or ten am. Nine am may sound like a normal breakfast time to some, but since I wake up at four-thirty this is well into my day. The green drink and flax seed make it easy to get to nine or ten with a manageable amount of hunger. Being a little hungry is okay, and it's so energizing! It also improves the taste of the food once you do eat.

I always prefer meals that are higher in clean fruits and veggies, lean protein sources, and carbs (mostly in the evening), that do not weigh me down. This is the mix that works for me and has nearly doubled the amount of energy I have each day. I encourage you to experiment and see what works for you!

In Moderation

The following foods, or food groups, are what I choose to consume in moderation. They are not part of the regular rotation.

Far from it, actually. Most have the propensity for blood sugar spikes and crashes, high fat or sugar concentrations, or somehow make me a little anxious. With that said, they can be fun on occasion!

- **Alcohol**: Yup, I went there. I used to have an alcoholic beverage once or twice a week, sometimes a bit more if I got together with friends on the weekend. IPA's were my beverage of choice, though I also enjoyed a nice glass of pinot noir or a Captain Morgan with cola. Two limes please! Unfortunately, the gluten in beer was slowing me down and adding on a few pounds, and the sugar in spirits and wine tended to spike my blood sugar then dip super low a few hours later. Now I save my sips for experiences and occasions where it feels right. As a bonus, now that I consume in moderation and I am eating clean, I need a lot less alcohol to get a buzz.

- **Coffee**: I love coffee, and I mean really, truly love a hot cup of the GOOD stuff! It increases my mental alertness, gives me a nice spike in energy, and now that I have discovered Bulletproof coffee (the butter coffee), I occasionally use it to curb my morning hunger. This is one of the choices, however, that I must consume in moderation. Coffee can upset my stomach if I drink it too often, crash my energy mid-day without a second cup, and occasionally gives me a bit of anxious impatience. If you are popping antacids just so you can enjoy your morning joe, you may want to reconsider the benefits. Also think about the crazy number of empty calories you are ingesting when you choose to drink your coffee via a double mocha, salted caramel, vente Frappuccino! If you do still drink coffee with regularity, check out Dave Asprey's Bulletproof line of products. I do feel less acidic when I chose these super clean beans.

- **Gluten**: Bread, flaky pastries, pizza, and many pastas are a super quick way to make me feel full and tired after a meal. While I have never been gluten-intolerant, this food choice has rarely been a good one for me. With that said, my occasional exceptions to the "no-gluten" guideline have been fun! In 2016, my son and I took a long road trip over the Holidays. We visited (in order), Pittsburgh PA, Rochester NY, Boston MA, Manhattan NY, and Washington DC. All amazing cities and we enjoyed the heck out of that experience! When we were in Boston, we visited a highly rated coffee shop in Harvard Square called Café Crema. (They closed in late 2018. So sad!) That morning was absolutely freezing, so we both ordered a hot cappuccino and an egg sandwich with ham and cheese. The coffee came out first, complete with the little crème artwork on top (such talent)! It was bold, hot, and full of flavor! Then the sandwiches came. Wow! Croissants baked right there in the café, farm fresh eggs spilling over the side, with generous amounts of sliced ham and cheese. To this day, I believe it was the best breakfast sandwich I have ever experienced. Well worth the gluten. No guilt attached.

Never! No Way!

This is the section where I may lose a few friends. I am going to pick on a few food groups that I have found didn't serve me and, I believe, probably won't serve you either. I promise that I am not getting judgmental here, and what you choose to ingest is completely up to you. I am simply sharing my opinions and supporting them with things I have experienced.

- **Diet Soda**: *"Ouch!"* Decades before I started this journey, I was anti-diet sodas for a few reasons. Personally, I didn't like the way they tasted. Yes, they were sweet and carbonated, but I couldn't stand the fake sugar aftertaste you get with artificial sweeteners. In addition, the chemicals that go into a diet drink are bad for your body, and your brain. The fact that they are zero calories, and give you a buzz, cannot make up for the fact that they can cause a series of health problems over time, including, but not limited to: spikes in blood sugar, increased risk of diabetes (yes, even without the real sugar!), high blood pressure, and weight gain (again, yes, even without the calories). Diet soda has also been linked to depression, skin conditions, digestive problems, kidney issues, even erosion of tooth enamel. The more I read about the impact of diet soda, the more I understand that the risk/reward doesn't add up.

- **"Fat Free" Processed Foods:** Ever since they were introduced, fat free food options have been all the rage. There are fat free crackers, frozen dinners, cookies, chips, and more. Unfortunately, removing the fat from foods means they had to increase other macro nutrients. That meant more sugar, flour, thickeners, chemicals, and salt. Fat free quickly became nutrition free. Leave them alone, and if you need a snack get the real deal.

- **Trans Fats**: Anything that includes trans fats is super inflammatory, and I diligently try to avoid them. Commercially fried foods, shortening, most partially hydrogenated vegetable oils, and non-dairy creamers are all on this list. A lot of bakery products (cookies, cakes, and Danishes) are also in this food group. It is difficult to buy salty snacks, or snacks of any kind, that was not baked or fried in one of these culprits. When I must have a salty crunchy snack, I look for something cooked in avocado or coconut oil. It's worth the extra two to three dollars I will spend. I am worth it, and so is my energy!

- **Refined carbohydrates (aka most processed, long shelf life foods)**: Crackers, instant potatoes, and a majority of commercially processed foods fall into this category. White flour spikes your glycemic index (not a good thing) and makes you crave it even more. Who needs those highs and lows? If you look at your grocery cart, and most of the food items are pre-packaged, have a long shelf life, and are super convenient options you may want to take a look at how much nutrition they are providing to you in the long term.

- **MSG and Aspartame**: The chemicals in these additives always, and I mean always, give me a debilitating headache. I read food labels now as much to make sure they lack these two culprits as I am scanning for protein quantities.

Fat in Food: Not all fats are bad for you!

News flash: Not all fats are the bad, must avoid at all costs offenders in most eating scenarios! Choosing the right fats, however, is the real key. We need fat in our diet for a variety of reasons, including giving our body energy, supporting cell growth, and helping us absorb essential nutrients. We require fat to survive! Ingesting the right ones can mean the difference between energy/weight loss, and lethargy/weight gain. Here are the fats that are now in my diet, followed by those I avoid:

Good Fats:
- Avocado (Whole, oil)
- Coconut Oil
- Olives and Extra Virgin Olive Oil
- MCT or Brain Octane Oil (Highly refined coconut oil. I love this!)
- Nuts (especially walnuts, pecans, raw almonds, pumpkin seeds)
- Fatty Fish (Salmon, Tuna, Mackerel, Halibut, Trout, Sardines)
- Cheese (in moderation, preferably from grass fed cows)
- Dark Chocolate
- Whole Eggs
- Chia Seeds

Bad Fats:
- Margarine (nasty): My sweet grandfather used to make a scene if a restaurant tried to serve him margarine. Can't say I blame him! Not one thing good about it!
- Packaged snack foods (exceptions are those cooked with good oils)
- Fried food (fried chicken, French fries, breaded and deep fried fish)

- Hydrogenated or partially hydrogenated vegetable oil (found in a ton of snack foods)
- Saturated Fats: Not only is this hard on the joints and can cause inflammation, it is also a major contributor to heart disease.
- Trans Fats: Found in fried foods, processed foods, cookies, donuts, and many other baked goods.

Now that you are good and hungry from reading about a plethora of food choices, let's switch to a topic that we literally cannot live without.

Water Works!

Over the last few decades water has become a new cool beverage choice for the on-the go, busy individual, increasing in demand exponentially over the years. This is great news! You see water everywhere. It is one of the top choices in a vending machine, many airports now have water stations available for dehydrated passengers, and entire rows are dedicated to bottled water choices in most shopping centers. Everyone seems to be carrying a water bottle of some kind, whether it is disposable (rethink that please!), or one of the high-tech hydro flasks now readily available. It was not like this at all when I was growing up, where soda and packaged sugar drinks were the typical go-to options. A lot has changed, and that's a good thing, because our bodies absolutely crave copious amounts of this liquid life changer!

According to WebMD, water is currently the second most popular beverage (behind soft drinks, unfortunately). We need water to hydrate and keep our bodies functioning, and for most of us the loss of water daily is greater than our cadence of replenishment. WebMD agrees. It goes on to say, *"Fluid losses occur continuously, from skin evaporation, breathing, urine, and stool, and these losses must be replaced daily for good health."*

I cannot overstate the importance of getting enough water in your daily Focus, Fit, and Fulfilled routine. I am just now understanding this, because for years I was in a near constant state of dehydration. My daily beverages were usually green tea in the morning, coffee at work, iced tea, a few token sips of water at lunch, another cup of coffee or tea to get me through the afternoon, then soy or almond milk at dinner. Unless it was Friday, and the milk was replaced by my favorite IPA. I usually drank water when I went to bed in part because I was so incredibly thirsty at the end of the day. Almost everything I was drinking was a diuretic (think, "makes me pee"), and I wasn't doing enough to replace the fluids I was losing. The impact was so stealth-like that I didn't make the connection until I switched my water habits around, but they included:

- Fatigue

- Headaches

- Severe muscle cramping, mostly in my feet
- Dry skin

Other side effects of not drinking enough clean water are:

- Increased risk of kidney stones
- High cholesterol
- Bad breath
- Aching joints
- Moodiness

The body needs water to perform its essential functions, including elimination, assimilating food, and maintaining healthy blood flow and organ function, just to name a few. Contrarily, the benefits of increasing your water consumption are plentiful, and I have felt the shift personally. They include:

- Mitigating hunger
- Reducing fatigue
- Flushing toxins
- Reducing constipation
- Helping nutrients and minerals assimilate
- Lubricating the joints
- Boosting skin health
- Regulating body temperature
- Maintaining healthy blood pressure
- Improving performance during exercise

How much water should you drink?

There are a wide variety of recommendations out there, with no universally accepted benchmark. The one that appears with the greatest consistency, however, is this: *Drink half of your body weight in ounces, or as much as you can and still feel comfortable.*

It's easy math. For a woman who is 128 pounds, that's 66 ounces of water a day. An average water bottle is twelve ounces, so that would be the equivalent of just over five bottles of water. (Please don't use disposable water bottles if you can help it. They are toxic to the environment, are clogging up our oceans, and have a horrible carbon footprint. I highly recommend a stainless steel, refillable bottle, such as a Hydro Flask. You can usually carry more ounces with you, and it keeps water cool most of the day!)

If you are already thinking there is no possible way to drink that much water in a day and still be productive (bathroom breaks do take some time), I recommend easing into increased consumption. If you are like I was, and water was a nice to have, not a need to have, then start by committing to drinking a twelve-ounce bottle by lunchtime and another twelve-ounce bottle before dinner. The benefits will be immediate, including a reduced (not eliminated) urge to snack, improved ability to focus, and balanced blood sugar. Yes, side effects include using the restroom more, but that will level off over time as your body adjusts. Once you get into the swing of this improved water intake, up it a little more each week until you reach your goal.

Now that we are hydrated, and well fed, let's add some physical movement to this new fitness regime. The good news is that this does not have to be complicated. All you have to do is move!

Just Move!

I've been an athlete my entire life. I remember as far back as five-years-old throwing a baseball into one of those pitch back nets and feeling the return volley smack crisply into my glove. I was hooked! Eventually, I wanted to do anything that included a ball, a net, a puck, or a court. I would play catch in the yard anytime I could convince my brothers to come outside with me. I rode my horse, Sahara, every day the weather allowed, often bareback with just a lead rope and a halter. I also loved playing a different kind of HORSE, with a basketball, challenging the neighborhood kids in our driveway. Little things like going to a Rochester Red Wing minor league baseball game with my dad and his work buddies, so he could show off my baseball knowledge, fill me with joyful memories. I was a runner too, and frequently ran in five and ten K's when I could. I even used to run a few miles before softball practice, on my own, just to warm up. I needed to move. I was always happier moving.

Exercise and Endorphins

Only in hindsight did I ever wonder why I was so drawn to sports and fitness, but now I believe I have it figured out. Besides the comradery and competition of team sports I was also hooked on the high produced by physical exertion! If being fit and having more energy weren't enough of a catalyst for movement, the addictive release of endorphins may be. That buzz you feel after a good workout, a long walk, or a nice hike in the mountains is simply amazing. The rush I used to feel after a hot, sweaty day in the sun at a tournament, or the gym workout that I almost put off but didn't. For me, that buzz seems to last all day and most certainly elevates my mood. Have you ever wondered why movement and working out feel so good?

It's the endorphins! According to Medicalnewstoday.com, *"Endorphins are chemicals produced naturally by the nervous system to cope with pain or stress. They are often called 'feel good' chemicals because they act as a pain reliever and happiness booster."* The site goes on to share that the name endorphin comes from the words "endogenous" (from the body) and "morphine" (opioid pain reliever). Essentially, a good workout has a similar, albeit natural, effect to taking the high inducing opioid medication, no prescription required. Said another way, it just feels good!

Besides the amazing moods created through consistent exercise, dedicating time to this pursuit also produces an increase of sustainable energy in my day. I get less brain fog and I am not nearly as quick to burn out when I squeeze in an early morning workout. I sleep better at night too and find it easier to eat cleaner during the day. And who can argue with the aesthetic results of consistent exercise?

To recap, working out feels amazing, releases endorphins that make you happy, gives you more energy to use during the day, and improves sleep at night. It's tough to argue against finding time for this critical element of a Focused, Fit, and Fulfilled lifestyle!

But I don't have time to exercise!

This, by far, is the most common excuse I have heard from individuals who are struggling to carve out time for a consistent workout. Their days are already "too full." They already have more commitments than they can handle. Going to the gym is too time consuming and inconvenient. There is just not enough energy in their body to layer on one more thing. I know these excuses well, because I have used them all.

If these reasons sound familiar, I would like to challenge you to think differently. In fact, I'm calling you out. If you have time for social media and Hulu/Netflix/Amazon Prime viewing binges, you have time to exercise. If you think about it, screen time is as much about watching other people pursue their dreams as it is "connecting" with those that mean something to you. The shows created for our consumption are the realization of someone else's vision, their big aspiration. Social media is filled with inspiring quotes and positive affirmations about how someone else was able to focus on what is important. Please know that I am not anti-social, or anti-streaming, but I am pro giving a rip about how you feel. Pro making *you* a priority. Like I said, if you have time for social every day you have time to work on you.

I am not advocating for a specific workout routine or "guaranteed to get you fit" set of exercises. They all work. There are hundreds of routines, gyms, apps, books, coaches, DVD's, websites, and classes you can take. This is about approach, mindset, belief in your ability to transform your body into something that will serve you, and all of those amazing goals you want to chase down. It's about getting out there and moving in a consistent, progressive way that enhances your energy, your focus, and the satisfaction you are getting out of your integrated life!

Why it's called an exercise "Routine"!

In my life, moving from inconsistent to consistent workouts was all about timing and approach. As you may remember, my old routine included getting up in the morning, making my green drink, getting back in bed, meditating on my goals, reading the news and my social media, and so on. By the time I was ready to move, I barely had time to let Nova out, quickly stretch, shower, and get to work. I could easily spend sixty to ninety minutes in bed "aligning" for the day, and I had a lot of excellent excuses for not working out: *I am stiff in the morning. It's too hard to get in a good workout so early. It's too cold in the morning. I don't have time. I don't want to drive to the gym. I'll start this weekend. I'll start when I get home tonight.*

Working out felt like a luxury, not an absolute must! I knew intuitively what the benefits of exercise were, but if it felt optional, I knew it would not happen with any degree of consistency. Like most of my changes I needed to push through this mental block and create another shift in my beliefs.

Exercise Paradigm Shift

From: *"I will work out when I have the time and energy to do so, and tomorrow is a great place to start."*

To: *"Working out 4-5 times a week is an integral part of my life! It's a must!"*

I knew that if I wanted to achieve the extraordinary goals I had envisioned I would need to find a way to significantly improve my exercise regimen. I simply had to find the time, had to make it a must. For me this was achieved through carving out a pocket of time in the morning. (Another benefit of being a morning person!) It was simple:

- I significantly reduced my morning "alignment" time to about thirty minutes. I still have my greens and I meditate, but everything else has either been reduced or eliminated. At the end of thirty minutes, there is now an alarm in my head saying, "Let's go!"
- I dress for a workout, grab Nova (which isn't hard, since she is my shadow in the morning), and go out to

the garage. One of the best decisions Andrew and I made was to invest in a home gym. I used to go to a local bootcamp, which also worked extremely well, but the home gym eliminated many of my former excuses, which is what I needed to get back on track. Our garage now has weights, benches, bands, and my favorite, a kick ass Assault Air Bike. It's similar to the bikes you see in the Cross-Fit Games and provides a wonderful resistance cardio workout.

- I get on the bike each morning and instead of listening to my favorite tunes I watch them on YouTube. The videos engage my waking up brain while my legs and arms get the blood flowing. I am ten minutes in before I even realize I am "working," though I have already achieved an elevated heart rate and a good sweat.

- After my body is nice and loose from the bike, I add a series of lunges, squats, barbell curls, shoulder stretches, whatever is on the agenda that day. (See the section on Two-Twenties below.) Forty minutes start to finish, and this can be reduced to thirty if you are just getting started or increased to an hour or more once you ramp up. I usually incorporate interval training so that I am mixing up the muscle groups I activate. Bottom line, whatever exercise you choose to reboot your fitness, pick one that you enjoy so that you can put the "routine" back in your exercise routine. Just move!

Exercise is incredibly addictive, and once you are in a pattern of frequent exertion you begin to crave it just as you do your morning beverage. If you currently lack a lot of movement in your life, this may be hard to believe, but it's true. The more you move the more you want to.

A Plethora of Workout Options

There are a wide, and I mean WIDE variety of fitness options out there. You can practice yoga, dance, lift weights, run, walk, swim, CrossFit, boot camps, basketball, skate, ski, or even do planks until your middle is as solid as a rock. For many of these, there are apps that will guide you and track your progress. Options are not the issue. It's about finding something you LIKE to do. What good is a workout routine if you loathe doing it and will find any excuse to avoid it? Not exactly the makings of a beautiful relationship! In general, fitness options fall into three categories. Find one that works for YOU!

Option 1: Structured gym time with a trainer or accountability partner(s). If you need the energy of being around others, if you crave comradery and community, joining a gym with structured classes (and then showing up!) might be right for you. Please know that not all gyms were created equal in terms of both assistance and people, however, once you are in a nice flow you will realize crazy cool physical and mental benefits, including the connection you will begin to feel with your fellow gym rats. Familiar options include, but are not limited to:

- CrossFit
- Orange Theory Fitness
- Bootcamp Style Gyms
- Bikrams Yoga (and other intense yoga practices)
- Beginners Yoga
- Boxing, Martial arts

Option 2: Home gym with a set routine. The beauty of having a home gym is that the commute to your workout space is reasonable, and nearly always traffic free! (As long as the walk from your bedroom to the space is free of obstructions.) Nevertheless, there is a lack of accountability and community that you might experience from regular visits to the gym. Still, with the right mindset, and a structured workout plan, this is a wonderful option. One that I employ today.

Working out at home doesn't have to be boring, or even freestyle. There are a wide variety of DVD sets that are fun to structure your routine around. (I have gone through P90X several times in the past. Thank you, Tony Horton!) YouTube also offers a wide variety of free exercise videos of all shapes and sizes. If you can stream it you can do it! The key here is that you have a plan. Exercising every day until you *feel* like you are done will probably not get the *peak* results you want.

The Two Twenties, plus Twenty-Percent More

My Grandfather, Arthur T. Burchard, used to tell me, *"Michelle, do everything they ask you to do, and just a little bit more. It's the little bit more that will get you noticed."* I am certain my Grandpa was referencing how to succeed in the workplace, and this concept served me well my entire career. I also believe this premise can be handily utilized in your fitness pursuit, especially if you are working out at home.

One of the hardest things about exercising on your own is the fact that there is no one there to push you. No coach, not the pressure to complete the workout with the rest of the group. Not even the guilt of *"Well shoot, I drove all this way I am going to get a good sweat in before I leave!"* When you are home, it is super easy to get a good workout started, then stop, just for a moment, to take clothes out of the dryer, water the plants you have been staring at as you stretched, make a quick call, or answer the *"where is my..."* query that inevitably comes from your spouse / partner / child / roommate / friend. It can be difficult to really push through to a peak level of exertion with all these inherent distractions! Difficult, but not impossible. How do you break through the limiting wall of ease and familiarity! I use two concepts, which I call "Two Twenty's" and "Twenty Percent More".

Two Twenty's

In the period leading up to, and while writing, this book, I exclusively worked out at home. While I do plan on going back to the gym later this year (I am ready to become a CrossFit Athlete!), exercising on my own allowed me to get to a place I needed to be. It all came together in our home gym in Southern California, where fortunately the weather is conducive to exercising outside much of the year. I break up my work out routine into two twenty-minute segments, and in most cases, it looks like this:

1. **First Twenty Minutes: Warming Up:** I spend the initial twenty minutes on some form of aerobic exercise and getting a deep stretch. This could include a fast walk with Nova, a light jog, or even jumping rope. My favorite by far is the getting on the Assault-style air bike we have in our gym, which provides resistance for my entire body and really elevates my heart rate. Best investment ever! I usually put my phone on the front of the bike and queue up a few Krewella videos on YouTube. Four songs in I am sweating like a fiend and ready for action! After the aerobic exercise, I get in some deep stretching exercises, which is important as you age. I focus on my entire body at first, then concentrate on the area(s) that I will be working on during the second "twenty."

2. **Second Twenty Minutes: Get Lifting!** Now that I have a good sweat on (don't forget to hydrate!), and my body is

nice and limber, I go into the second twenty-minute segment of my routine. It always includes some form of weights, stretch bands, or body weight resistance exercises, working my muscles and adding more lean mass over time. There is no reason to lose muscle tone as you age! Just ask the 50+ Tony Horton of P90X fame! I rotate which body segments I am working on and can easily get a good burn when lifting weights, doing pushups, body weight squats, planks, planks with movement, and using those progressive resistance bands. I lift in increasingly heavier sets, starting out at a comfortable weight and pushing myself a little at the end.

3. **Just a Little Bit More**: This is where the *twenty-percent more* comes in. Let's use as an example working out my biceps and triceps. I start with a set of bicep curls that I can do easily, fifteen to twenty reps, take a break, switch to triceps, etc. When I get into the progressively heavier sets, and I sense it would be completely normal to stop there, feeling satisfied, I ask my body to do *twenty-percent more*. Every time! Twenty-percent more weight, twenty-percent more reps, sometimes both.

It is this "little bit more" that has taken me from "better" shape to "best shape ever!" I will be ready for CrossFit this fall! Bottom line, if you choose to workout at home, please make sure you have a plan that pushes you beyond your comfort zone a bit if you want to see real results.

Option 3: Exercise via Play and Connection! The final option is to have some fun, connect with others, and still exert yourself physically. Working out via play! Exercise does not have to be in a sweaty gym with clothing that you are not comfortable wearing out in public yet. It can be done in a dress, with skates, on a court, in a pool, in your bathing suit, in cleats, or even in your casual clothes with a nice pair of walking shoes. I am referring to, of course, the amazing experiences of dancing, ice or roller skating, swimming, walking, hiking, playing basketball, soccer, cricket, volleyball, biking, and so much more!

Having spent my life as an athlete, I just adore the comradery, and achievement, that comes with this type of activity. It's a wonderful high to finish a game, having won or lost, and feel like you left it all on the proverbial court. You can feel this same euphoria when you learn a new dance, take a Zumba class, roller skate with friends, or even take that evening stroll with your BFF. Things like bike rides, walks, and hiking have the added benefit of being able to see new sites and connect with nature, which is abundant here in sunny California and most states.

Walking Works Wonders!

Speaking of walking, I am always impressed when I see an elderly couple walking together in what appears to be a daily routine. They seem to have a spring in their step and are clearly enjoying the process. They also typically appear to be on the fit side of the equation, lean and standing straight. (Cause and effect?) If all of the workout suggestions listed above seem too drastic a change from where you are now, walking is a wonderful place to start. Getting out of that comfy chair every day may be tough at first, but the benefits are incredibly clear, and you are going to eventually look forward to this new daily routine!

If Exercise via Play is your choice for movement, that's wonderful! The bottom line is that to be in a Focused, Fit, and Fulfilled lifestyle you have to include some form of intentional exercise in your day. Just move! It will be worth every drop of sweat!

On the Road Again!

As a final topic, I would like to cover how to keep the momentum going if you are a frequent traveler. There's no reason why you must start and stop your momentum because you are in hotels and conference rooms! When I travel, I always pack some workout clothes, and I either hit the hotel gym or I exercise in my room. I created this efficient, and incredibly effective, routine when I am on the road, and it only takes twenty minutes:

- Walk in place, knees comfortably high, for about three to five minutes. Great way to get the blood flowing.
- Stretch all my major muscle groups. This is also a nice time to say some meditative mantras.
- Now that I am warmed up, I switch to my twenties:

- 20 body weight squats
- 20 push-ups (use the extra blanket or a few towels. You don't know where that floor has been)!
- 20 alternating toe touches
- 20 lunges
- 20 crunches (floor or bed)
- 20 chair dips

- As I increased my fitness level, I would repeat this set two or three times, but even once is enough to ward off any muscle or energy loss from my travels. It really works!

As you can see, there are a ton of ways to integrate working out and movement into your life. Fitness is achievable for everyone, but it needs to be exciting, not a chore. Shift what you are doing until you find something you get enthusiastic about and keep at it until it becomes a must. You can do this!

Stretch To Connect, Stretch To Decompress

One of the practices that has supported my Focused, Fit, and Fulfilled lifestyle is my practice of stretching every morning and night. Maybe it's because my body is less flexible than it was at twenty. Maybe it's just a great way to ramp up my energy in the morning, and a wonderful way to decompress before bed. Either way, I love the effects of this part of my day.

Did you ever wonder why stretching feels so good? Why athletes stretch before an event? It has a lot to do with both range of motion in your joints and keeping your muscles long and flexible. Without stretching you are more prone to that slow and stealthy decline that is associated with aging, along with the reduced mobility that may come as the years advance.

Further defined, range of motion (ROM) is the ability to move joints in a smooth pattern. Stretching your muscles allows them to remain flexible, strong, and able to support the joints they are attached to. Often, when someone has arthritis or wear and tear on a joint, the recommendation is to strengthen the surrounding muscles, so they can better support said joint.

Muscles that are not stretched regularly become short and tight, which leaves us, and the athletes mentioned above, more prone to injury. There's good news, though. When ROM and muscle length decreases with age, inactivity, or injury, there are many excellent ways to get things loosened up again.

Forms of Stretching

The two most common forms of stretching are:

1. **Static**: The most recognizable type of stretching, where a specific position is held for a period of time, with the intent

to lengthen, or loosen, the muscle. For maximum results, the position is repeated several times with gradual increases in tension.

2. **Dynamic**: Two different techniques fall under the category of dynamic stretching: Active and Ballistic. Think of Active stretching as moving a joint through the full range of motion in a fluid manner, such as arm circles. This type of movement allows additional blood to flow into the area, thus warming it up and preparing for additional demands. Ballistic stretching is a bit more taxing, and if not properly warmed up you can risk injury. An example of Ballistic stretching could be a rapid series of short squats where you bounce back at the bottom of the motion. This also allows blood to flow to the area and prepares for more intense exercise demands.

I encourage you to use a combination of all of the possibilities listed above, but here's the key. Stretching is not supposed to hurt. If you begin to move in a way that causes pain, stop immediately and seek out advice from your health care provider. Keep in mind the distinct difference between pain and stiffness though. Stiffness is something we should gradually work through. As we age, even with a fit lifestyle, our muscles and joints begin to deteriorate. Stretching increases blood flow and circulation, allows us to maintain a healthy range of motion, and keeps us mobile and active.

As an athlete, I have long been a fan of the inherent benefits of stretching. Now, as an over-fifty, still rocking and rolling exercise enthusiast, I can see and feel those positive aspects even more. I have incorporated stretching into lifestyle both in the morning through "Stretch to Connect," and at night when I "Stretch to Decompress."

How I Stretch

While there are dozens of ways to properly stretch, listed below are the methods I use: *Please note, if you are recovering from an injury or surgery, please follow the recommendations of your health care practitioner.*

Remembering that stretching should never cause pain, I still try to significantly increase my range of motion with each session. I love the delight I feel when I am able to go from creaky and stiff to limber and fluid. Here's how:

Round One

1. For each stretching position I move my body to the point where I can begin to feel the resistance.
2. I hold in that position, breathing normally for about 5 seconds.
3. I return to a neutral position and switch sides (if applicable).
4. Working through a variety positions, I run through each stretch one time each before moving on to

Round Two. This usually gets me warmed up and ready for more.

Round Two

1. Going back to the same series of stretches, I hold the first pose for 2-3 seconds.
2. I then take a deep breath, holding the same pose.
3. As I exhale the deep breath, I try to ease just a bit farther into each pose. Breathe in, hold, breathe out, stretch a bit more.
4. Repeat 3-4 times and I end up getting a really deep stretch in each position. It works wonders!

I have always been mesmerized by the apparent peace and tranquility of a group doing Tai Chi. The flowing movements, the centered look of stillness, and the incredible range of motion displayed is inspirational. I have also personally experienced Qi Gong, another ancient form of stretching and connecting. I discovered Qi Gong when I was struggling with sleep, before I recognized that the sleeplessness was due to an overactive mind and a boatload of stress. While these practices are both wonderfully structured ways to move, any form of stretching is going to serve the goal of staying flexible.

Stretch to Connect

As I started planning my Focus, Fit, and Fulfilled lifestyle, I knew I wanted to formally incorporate stretching into my daily practice. I start every morning with meditation and visualizing my goals and outcomes for the day. Because that is typically done in a resting seated position, after I warm up the mind and the soul I need to warm up and prepare the body. But to continue the positive momentum and vibes, I seek to further connect when I stretch. As I stretch, I let the flow of gratitude take precedence in my thoughts. I am grateful for the ability to move, for the way my legs, back, arms, etc. feel. I am grateful for a new day, for the opportunities in my life, for the heartwarming relationships, friends and family, for the great experiences I know I will have. After feeling gratitude, I purposely seek to connect with my inner being. I don't always say anything; I strive to feel the connection to my soul. "We've got this, don't we?" "Let's make this day beautiful." Going through my stretches, feeling gratitude and connection, always, always always leaves me in a fantastic mood, ready to begin.

Stretch to Decompress

Stretching in the evening is like the morning routine, except for my focus. This time is essentially a way to kick off my hour of winding down, so I use it to transition from a task centered, high achieving mentality, to a slower-paced mode focused on gratitude. I run through the day and think about all the things I am grateful for, the things that went well and made me smile. I briefly touch on those topics that could have been improved. I remind myself that even failure is a part of the learning journey, while giving myself permission to let it go. Finally, I vibe love to everyone in my life, sending hope of a beautiful, happy day tomorrow. Ending this practice on love is a fantastic way to go to bed filled with peace.

Five Elements of Fitness, Conclusion

It is my sincere hope that you will find a way to incorporate each of the five elements into your life, in ways that work for you alone. We all have these wonderful bodies, and precious minds, that we get to test and adjust with; so be curious, try different things and see what works, and never forget that the end goal is to feel good as often as you can. Which leads us to our final pillar, the wonderful, and sometimes elusive, quest for fulfillment.

Section 3: FULFILLMENT

"Success without fulfillment is the ultimate failure."

– Tony Robbins

We have reached the final chapters of Focused, Fit, and Fulfilled after 50, and I have to say, I am honored to have made this journey with you. That, in and of itself, was worth the months, weeks, days, and hours putting this together. Writing these words, having traversed all of the steps that led to this point, sharing with you how this new approach has already changed the joy in my heart, feels precious, memorable, and satisfying. Deep appreciation is being felt right now for the forces that brought us to this!

Now that we are here, what's next? How do we really lean into the ability to allow fulfillment to increase in our lives? It is both easier than you think and potentially one of the most difficult puzzles to solve. Task completion and goal achievement do not automatically result in a feeling of fulfillment, especially for the type A overachievers amongst us. We are so wired to strive towards a goal that the tendency, once said goal is reached, is to briefly acknowledge the achievement, accept congratulations with humility, and immediately look for the next mountain to climb. Or worse, that immediate inclination to pivot to "*I'm not worthy of this moment*" and try to downplay the achievement. Why not accept the congratulations with a simple "*thank you,*" and revel in the sensation for a bit? This was a lesson I had to teach myself, and it took some time!

What is Fulfillment?

Fulfillment, I believe, is so much more than realizing the physical manifestation of a goal. For me, that sense of fulfillment, or "*the achievement of something desired,*" is reached when I consistently **feel** that which I am seeking, long before it is physically represented in my life. When I am satisfied with my progress on the journey each small step uplifts me. Even when the choices I made did not necessarily move me forward, the fact that I was at least making choices, that I still had the courage to take risks and challenge the process, filled my heart with same sense of gratification. It's not the achievement of the goal that brings me the most joy, it's *becoming who I need to be to reach the goal I have in mind.*

"But if it goes to hell at least I know I tried."

– SKAAR "Higher Ground" song

The following brief sections describe how I have reached a place where I feel fulfilled on a consistent basis. It is my resolute belief that it is achievable for everyone, and that this sensation is intertwined with your focus and how you approach the physical energy in your body.

Love the Journey!

"Life is a journey, not a destination."

– Ralph Waldo Emerson

Before I started the expedition I have shared throughout this book, I had been working diligently towards that day when the home, the relationship, and the abundance would all fall into place. I wasn't really enjoying the process, instead I was pushing, pushing, pushing! I woke up each day to race towards what was next. I stressed myself out, thinking more effort would equal more results and a quicker path to the finish line. My happiness was contingent upon the physical manifestation of my goals, and mostly I just felt their absence. The big difference from where I was then to where I am today is that I realize happiness is not something I had to chase, or something to wait for. Happiness was mine to hold right here, right now.

To really allow happiness to seep into my current circumstances, I had to realize that is located along the path, not just at the destination. It is not a static entity waiting at the end of the race, like a shiny medal you receive when you cross the finish line. Joy is in the moments you find as your focused, peaceful mind leads you along the way.

As I write these final chapters, Andrew, Nova, and I are a day away from one of our epic road trips from Los Angeles to Rochester NY. We are both so excited (I'm sure Nova is too). It is not simply because we will be sitting in my mom's backyard in a few days, or that we will be visiting family, friends, and taking a break. We are just as jazzed about the 2400 miles that we will need to navigate to get there. We have always enjoyed our road trips, and the scenic journeys are a huge part of the reason why.

We love the moment we pull out of the driveway early in the morning, counting down from five as our trip begins. We feel enthusiasm every time we cross a state line and relish the dining opportunities we find along the way. We both make new playlists (thank goodness we have a similar taste in music), listen to podcasts, and get through at least one spy thriller on CD. It is the cumulative effect of these moments that make the thirty-eight-hour road trip worth every mile.

In similar fashion, I have learned that pursuing a goal, even one as monumental as my dream home on the ranch, is as much about the steps along the path, as it is the eventual achievement. Finding the perfect place on Zillow, recommended by a dear friend, was a wonderful step. Knowing that shifting my focus and fitness would take me closer, priceless. But it was also smaller moments that mattered, like making a connection with the delightful owner of the property and visiting them over the holidays. We are going back again soon, and I know it will not feel like "but it's not mine yet," it will resonate as "almost there." That's enjoying the journey.

Have you ever stopped to consider whether you are allowing, and I do believe it is a state of allowing, the joy of the journey to seep into your being? This can be achieved simply by slowing down and taking the time to honor who you are. Take pride in the efforts you have taken to this point and the courage you exuded to even pursue a change. Not everyone chooses to venture out in this way, and for that alone you should feel pretty good.

If the only thing you get out of this final section is to feel better along the path to your goals, and to slow down and soak in the majesty of life from time to time, then all of this will be well worth it. Keep up the amazing work, you! And please remember that you, and only you, can vibe that appreciation for your own journey. While it is always nice to feel the approval and gratitude of others, we need to give this gift to ourselves and not depend on the endorsement of another to allow this joy. Counting on another for approval gives away all of our power.

"It is not the critic who counts; not the man who points out how the strong man stumbles, or where the doer of deeds could have done better. The credit belongs to the man who is actually in the arena, whose face is marred by dust and sweat and blood..."

– Theodore Roosevelt

One other way to enjoy the journey is to vibe what I call "Infinite Love." Vibing means radiating, sending out, or otherwise exuding from your core that which is good inside of you. I often silently vibe infinite love in the most routine places, believing it impacts those I am sending it to just as it is filling my heart with joy. There is no limit to the places, people, or things you can direct love to. (That's why it's called infinite!) Some of my common ones are radiating love for:

- the process
- my imperfect self
- the victories
- the failures
- epic moments
- the mundane tasks
- the kind individuals I meet along the way
- the people too caught up in their own space to notice

- those who love me back
- those who couldn't care less
- the trees that clean our air and provide us shade and beauty
- the animals that love us unconditionally
- friends that never seem to forget the good inside of me, even when I am not that good
- even the drivers on the busy highways I traverse so often

Vibing this kind of love, without conditions or requirements, is a sure way to enjoy every step on the road to what you seek, and it helps put into context the beauty of the achievement once you get there. Because, after all, feeling joy as often as we can is a big part of this process.

> *"It's not just that your purpose is joy, it is that you are joy. You are love and joy and freedom and clarity expressing. Energy-frolicking and eager. That's who you are."*
>
> – Abraham-Hicks

Another important technique to keep more joy in your life is to watch the way you talk about yourself. Your word choices have more impact than you may imagine, even if those words are said in modesty or parody.

Watch Your Language!

Back in the day, it was a normal response for my mom or dad to say, "watch your language!" if, for some strange reason, I slipped and said something as egregious as "sucks" or "crap." My mom was especially diligent about the words we chose to use, even with our friends and each other. I used to tease my closest buddies all the time, as they did me, and if my mom was around she would interrupt us and express, *"Please don't say negative things about each other. Even if you're joking, there is a small part of that person that starts to believe what you are saying."* Then, she pressed us to say three nice things about the other person, which as a teenager often sounded like *"I like your shoelaces."* Mom knew the power of words and encouraged us to consider others when we spoke. She recognized that there was a part of every heart that was dinged when unkind words were spoken, and just as positive affirmations can ingrain optimistic behaviors, so can negative beliefs with repeated messaging.

I remember, decades ago, picking up my son from daycare in the private home of Mrs. Smith (real name withheld.). She watched four or five toddlers at the same time and was a blessing to me. Andrew loved going there! The only small downside was that another toddler there, we will call him Jon, was always into some sort of mischief. He was a high energy, rambunctious boy who didn't listen well, which in hindsight is not unusual for a toddler. Without judgment I want to share the following story.

One day I was picking up Andrew and having a chat with Mrs. Smith and Jon's mother. Jon's mom, a hardworking businesswoman who was always very nice to me, was telling Mrs. Smith about her challenges with Jon at home. "*He's always in trouble. I can never really trust him to be alone, not even for a few minutes. He's either breaking something, making a mess, or putting something in his mouth he shouldn't. He's a bad little boy quite a bit!*" This venting session went on for a good five minutes.

While this is a little sad, and I felt for Jon's mother, what broke my heart was looking over Mrs. Smith's shoulder into the den, just beyond where we were talking. There was Jon, sitting on the floor with a few toys, and while his back was to us, I could clearly see that his ear was tilted in the direction of our conversation. I desperately wanted to tell Jon's mother to stop. Just stop. Say something nice! How much of her language was causing, or reinforcing, the image that Jon was a "bad little boy?" Would it have helped if she had told stories about how smart he was? Or kind? Or good with his toys, his friends, his food, something! Anything! Words matter!

I am fortunate to have a son who is kind, great with his friends, and sweet to his grandparents. He is also smart and awesome at taking tests. Was this solely a result of his natural ability? Or did the fact that we talked about how taking tests was kind of like a game, a challenge, a chance to show how much you learned impact his ability. Bring it on! Don't get me wrong, most parents look back and play the 20/20 hindsight game, and I do too.

Was I too lax? Should I have made him play an instrument growing up? (He loves music so much, and I occasionally regret that I did not give him this foundation.) The bottom line is that I did the best I could, as all parents do (even yours!), and I raised a kind, smart, considerate, driven young man. I could not be more grateful, or proud.

Be Nice to Yourself!

Refraining from saying unkind things about others is one thing, but have you ever really paid attention to how you speak to and about yourself? Have you ever listened to the words you use when describing who you are, what you are doing, or how you feel? Words really do matter!

Have you ever said any of the following?

- I have always been low energy. It's the way I am wired.
- My family is big boned, so it's kind of hard for me to lose weight.
- I'm not good at math!
- I am not artistic. I can't even color inside the lines!
- I am not a morning person!
- I am not a night owl and can barely think after eight pm.
- Things rarely work out for me.
- I'm unlucky.

- When things start to go well, I always find a way to screw it up!
- I am not that pretty/handsome.
- I'll never find a partner that is kind to me.
- I seem to attract all the mean ones.

"Don't argue for your limitations."

– Abraham-Hicks

As the Genie in Aladdin famously said, *"Your wish is my command!"* Words do matter. If we repeatedly say unkind things to and about ourselves, those thoughts become hard wired into our identity. We seek to match the reality we have set for ourselves, even if that reality doesn't match what we want in life. If you tell everyone, "I am not a morning person" what are the chances you can start a new health routine that includes an early morning workout session? If you say, "I'm not good at math," what are the chances you can get your finances in order?

Why do people speak negatively about themselves? There is a fine line between humility: *"Oh, thank you, but my team really did the heavy lifting,"* and self-defeating language that turns into a belief system: *"I'm surprised it worked out, actually. That's not typical for me. Usually something goes wrong at the last minute."*

I too have fallen into this trap, but now I am good at catching myself. As an example, a few weeks ago, I talked to my editor about this book. Near the beginning of the conversation I said, *"And I know a lot of other people are writing books like this right now, but…*" I caught myself immediately and corrected, "*You know, I'm not going to say that anymore. That sounded a bit self-defeating.*" She caught it too and offered, "*Yeah, let's not do that.*" When you know the power of language you can become astute at watching out for words and phrases that simply do not empower you.

I challenge you to spend a week listening to how you speak about yourself. Both the words you say out loud to others and the *internal, non-verbal thoughts you think* to yourself. After spending a week passively listening, challenge yourself to spend the next week proactively eliminating all negative statements and intentionally replace them with positive ones. Become someone who knows their worth. Try these on for size:

- I always find a way!
- Things always work out somehow!
- I am a lucky person in general!
- Good things always seem to find their way to me!
- Abundance comes easily to me!
- I am surrounded by kind, positive people!
- I seem to draw good people to me.
- I am on my way to phenomenal results.
- I intuitively know what's best for my life.
- I am a kind individual.
- I laugh a lot!
- I feel loving energy around me all the time!

Also know that you are worthy *right now*, not just when you achieve your goal. You are worthy of:

- The Job
- The Recognition
- The Respect
- The Love
- The Faith
- The Loyalty
- The Warmth
- The Partnership
- The Support
- The Belief
- The Money
- The Success
- The Home
- The Appreciation
- Infinite Love

Finally, don't give too much power to what others think or say. In these days of social media trolls, negative press junkies, and those who are unhappy and trying to drag you down, or even people that just don't agree with you, it is far too easy to get sucked into believing the opinions of others. When I was growing up, someone could decide they didn't agree with me and they would tell ten to twenty of their friends. Massive scandal at school! Now people can post, often anonymously, words intentionally intended to hurt and reach thousands. I don't understand why, but it's out there. Personally, I have difficulty even posting a negative Yelp review because I know that my post may hurt someone's feelings. (So, I usually don't. Sorry fellow Yelp users!) If you give in to the criticism or intentional provocation of others, you will soon find yourself behaving in ways that are not organic to who you really are. Don't give it a second thought, and don't engage. You know who the most intoxicating people in the world are? The kind, self-confident people who are not vibing how much they need approval and couldn't give a flip about what others are saying.

Small Moments

One of the biggest lessons of my life so far, an epiphany that opened the door to immense amounts of happiness and gratitude, was the concept of really recognizing and appreciating the small moments in life that made me smile. For years, decades really, I believed that true peace and fulfillment would come when I achieved something big. The promotion, the new home or car, reaching an ideal weight, or finding the perfect partner. Looking back, I realize that the memories that warm my heart the most are not those felt at the finish line, but those little moments in between and along the way. While finishing the race, getting a raise, and falling in love are all wonderful achievements, life for me has been more about:

- The glance that made my heart jump and my eyes smile in return
- The kind words my son told me, expressing appreciation for my parenting
- Sitting in the courtyard with new neighbors that I felt an instant connection with
- Finding moments to laugh every day with Adam and Jim when they were onboard ships and appreciating the meaningful conversations with Dustin when our contracts overlapped. (Couldn't have done it without all of you!)
- Walking the Tennessee property with my best friend and the dogs on a crisp fall afternoon
- Watching one of our new ships come into port for the very first time
- Pizza with Jennifer and the girls, reliving stories already told hundreds of times
- Laughing with my brothers as we gave my dad a hard time about his love of the Yankees
- Making up silly words with my mom and my Aunt Sue, usually to express how we spoke to our dogs. (dee tee booties!)

Even as I write these words I smile inside as each memory evokes a corresponding feeling of warmth and joy. You may notice that not one of these sentiments reflected momentous occasions or extraordinary achievements. Don't get me wrong, those are fun too and totally worth pursuing. For me it really was time, though, to spend less energy focused on that which I had not yet achieved, and more time feeling appreciation for the little things that truly make a life worth living. Being able to give myself a break and recognize that so many amazing things have happened in my life already was a real key to lasting joy, and yes, a Fulfilled life. To all of those I have mentioned above, and the hundreds not mentioned who have impacted my life in joyous ways, I say simply "thank you."

Conclusion, For Now!

I hope you enjoyed reading *Focused, Fit, and Fulfilled After 50!* It was a dream fulfilled writing it, and a privilege testing these concepts out myself. The words I would love to leave you with are quite simple, but they mean a lot to me.

Please remember to:

- Have a goal that you can put 100% of your effort into. A goal that lifts your spirits and fills your heart with joy. A goal that is not contingent on the approval or actions of others.
- Explore the world around you now, not when you retire!
- Love yourself now. Don't wait until you achieve that which you pursue.
- Achievement is not what makes you worthy. You are worthy right now.
- Your best relationship can be with yourself. Honoring who you are, the soul inside, the great choices, and the moments of being fully human.

- Clarity, purpose, and joy are more important than material things. Find these and the rest is easy.

Also remember that while financial success and abundance are wonderful to have, money alone will not provide the deep level of peace and joy so many of us seek. It is a wonderful vehicle to take you there, yes, but it is not the destination. I leave you for now with one final quote, this time from my all-time favorite author Ayn Rand. In **Atlas Shrugged,** her prolific novel, one of her protagonists, Francisco d'Anconia, shared this poignant thought on this topic:

> *"Money is only a tool. It will take you wherever you wish, but it will not replace you as the driver. Money will not purchase happiness for the man who has no concept of what he wants. Money will not give him a code of values, if he's evaded the knowledge of what to value, and it will not give him a purpose, if he's evaded the choice of what to seek."*
>
> – Francisco d'Anconia, in *Atlas Shrugged* by Ayn Rand

Be the driver of your own life, and enjoy the scenes that life presents along the way.

Much love, and warm regards to you all!

Michelle

Made in the
USA
Columbia, SC